P9-EDE-718

WITHDRAWN
UTSA Libraries

Essays presented to
CHARLES WILLIAMS

Essays presented to
CHARLES
WILLIAMS

Contributors

DOROTHY SAYERS

J. R. R. TOLKIEN

C. S. LEWIS

A. O. BARFIELD

GERVASE MATHEW

W. H. LEWIS

Essay Index Reprint Series

 BOOKS FOR LIBRARIES PRESS
FREEPORT, NEW YORK

Copyright 1947 by
Oxford University Press.

Reprinted 1972 by arrangement.

Library of Congress Cataloging in Publication Data
Main entry under title:

Essays presented to Charles Williams.

    (Essay index reprint series)
    Bibliography: p.
    1. Literature--Addresses, essays, lectures.
I. Williams, Charles, 1886-1945. II. Sayers,
Dorothy Leigh, 1893-1957.
[PN36.W5 1972]   809   77-142623
ISBN 0-8369-2768-0

PRINTED IN THE UNITED STATES OF AMERICA
BY
NEW WORLD BOOK MANUFACTURING CO., INC.
HALLANDALE, FLORIDA 33009

PREFACE

IN this book the reader is offered the work of one professional author, two dons, a solicitor, a friar, and a retired army officer; if he feels disposed to complain of hotch-potch (which incidentally is an excellent dish; consult the *Noctes Ambrosianae*) I must reply that the variety displayed by this little group is far too small to represent the width of Charles Williams's friendships. Nor are we claiming to represent it. Voices from many parts of England—voices of people often very different from ourselves—would justly rebuke our presumption if we did. We know that he was as much theirs as ours: not only, nor even chiefly, because of his range and versatility, great though these were, but because, in every circle that he entered, he gave the whole man. I had almost said that he was at everyone's disposal, but those words would imply a passivity on his part, and all who knew him would find the implication ludicrous. You might as well say that an Atlantic breaker on a Cornish beach is 'at the disposal' of all whom it sweeps off their feet. If the authors of this book were to put forward any claim, it would be, and that shyly, that they were for the last few years of his life a fairly permanent nucleus among his *literary* friends. He read us his manuscripts and we read him ours: we smoked, talked, argued, and drank together (I must confess that with Miss Dorothy Sayers I have seen him drink only tea: but that was neither his fault nor hers).

Of many such talks this collection is not unrepresentative. The first three essays are all on literature, and even on one aspect of literature, the narrative art. That is natural enough. His *All Hallows' Eve* and my own *Perelandra* (as well as Professor Tolkien's unfinished sequel to the *Hobbit*) had all been read aloud, each chapter as it was written. They owe a good deal to the hard-hitting criticism of the circle. The problems of narrative as such—seldom heard of in modern critical writings—were constantly before our minds. The last two essays are historical. Father Mathew's bears on an aspect of the Middle Ages which always seemed to Williams of deep significance and which had, indeed, been the common interest that first brought him and me together. The final essay carries us to seventeenth-century France. My brother's lifelong interest in the reign of

Louis XIV was a bond between Williams and him which no one had foreseen when they first met. Those two, and Mr. H. V. D. Dyson of Merton, could often be heard in a corner talking about Versailles, *intendants*, and the *maison du roy*, in a fashion with which the rest of us could not compete. Between the literary and the historical essays stands Mr. Barfield's work, which is literary and historical at once. We had hoped to offer the whole collection to Williams as what the Germans call a *Festschrift* when peace would recall him from Oxford to London. Death forestalled us; we now offer as a memorial what had been devised as a greeting.

Something must here be said to those who may ask 'Who was Charles Williams?' He had spent most of his life in the service of the Oxford University Press at Amen House, Warwick Square, London. He was a novelist, a poet, a dramatist, a biographer, a critic, and a theologian: a 'romantic theologian' in the technical sense which he himself invented for those words. A romantic theologian does not mean one who is romantic about theology but one who is theological about romance, one who considers the theological implications of those experiences which are called romantic. The belief that the most serious and ecstatic experiences either of human love or of imaginative literature have such theological implications, and that they can be healthy and fruitful only if the implications are diligently thought out and severely lived, is the root principle of all his work. His relation to the modern literary current was thus thoroughly 'ambivalent'. He could be grouped with the counter-romantics in so far as he believed untheologized romanticism (like Plato's 'unexamined life') to be sterile and mythological. On the other hand, he could be treated as the head of the resistance against the moderns in so far as he believed the romanticism which they were rejecting as senile to be really immature, and looked for a coming of age where they were huddling up a hasty and not very generous funeral. He will not fit into a pigeon-hole.

The fullest and most brilliant expression of his outlook is to be found in his mature poetry, and especially in *Taliessin through Logres* and *The Region of the Summer Stars*. As I have in preparation a much longer study of these works, I must here content myself with saying that they seem to me, both for the soaring and gorgeous novelty of their technique and for their

profound wisdom, to be among the two or three most valuable
books of verse produced in the century. Their outstanding
quality is what I would call glory or splendour; a heraldic
brightness of colour, a marble firmness of line, and an arduous
exaltation. The note struck is very unlike that of the Nineteenth
Century, and equally unlike that of most moderns. It is the
work of a man who has learned much from Dante (the Dante
of the *Paradiso*) and who might be supposed (though in fact he
had not) to have learned much from Pindar. If its extreme
difficulty does not kill it, this work ought to count for much in
the coming years. I am speaking only of his mature work. He
found himself late as a poet and in his earlier poems I, for one,
do not see any promise of what he finally became.

He is best known by his criticism. I have learned much from
it—particularly from *The Figure of Beatrice* and *Poetry at Present*.
But it is distressing that many people, on hearing the name
Williams, should think chiefly or only of *The English Poetic
Mind*, or even of his criticism at all, for it is probably the
least valuable part of his work. Those who find the poetry too
difficult would be much better advised to turn to the novels.

*The Greater Trumps, War in Heaven, Many Dimensions, The
Place of the Lion, Descent into Hell*, and *All Hallows' Eve* present,
under the form of exciting fantasy, some of the most important
things Williams had to say. They have, I think, been little
understood. The frank supernaturalism and the frankly blood-
curdling episodes have deceived readers who were accustomed
to seeing such 'machines' used as toys and who supposed that
what was serious must be naturalistic—or, worse still, that what
was serious could not be gay. And in the earlier stories, it must
be allowed, there were technical defects which stand between
us and the author's meaning. There was a good deal of over-
writing, of excess in the descriptions and, in dialogue, of a false
brilliance. But this was overcome in the later work and in this
respect the distance between *War in Heaven* and the sobriety
and strength of the *Descent* and the *Eve* is a remarkable witness
to his continually growing, self-correcting art. But the imagination and the spiritual insight had been there from the beginning;
and it is these that always justify both the infernal and the
paradisal turns of the story. They are never in excess of
what the author most seriously intends. Hence the cathartic
value of these fantasies. We are not likely in real life to meet an

objective *succubus* as Wentworth does in *Descent into Hell*, nor to
be haunted by a pterodactyl as Damaris Tighe is haunted in *The
Place of the Lion*. But those who, like Wentworth, are following
what seems to be love into the abyss of self-love will know in
the end what the *succubus* means; and the frivolously academic
who 'do research' into archetypal ideas without suspecting that
these were ever anything more than raw material for doctorate
theses, may one day awake, like Damaris, to find that they are
infinitely mistaken.

I first heard of Charles Williams a great many years ago when
a man who was sitting next to me at dinner (Dr. R. W. Chap-
man) asked me if I had read any of his novels. He described
them as 'spiritual shockers'. I was interested and made a
mental note that this was an author to be looked into, but did
nothing about it. A few years later I spent an evening at
Exeter College in the rooms of Mr. N. K. Coghill. He was full
of a book he had just read called *The Place of the Lion*, by Charles
Williams. No man whom I have ever met describes another
man's work better than Mr. Coghill (his descriptions of Kafka
always seemed to me better even than Kafka himself) and I
went home with his copy of *The Place of the Lion*. Twenty-four
hours later I found myself, for the first time in my life, writing
to an author I had never met to congratulate him on his book.
By return of post I had an answer from Williams, who had
received my letter when he was on the point of writing a similar
letter to me about my *Allegory of Love*. After this, as may be
supposed, we soon met and our friendship rapidly grew inward
to the bone.

Until 1939 that friendship had to subsist on occasional
meetings, though, even thus, he had already become as dear to
all my Oxford friends as he was to me. There were many
meetings both in my rooms at Magdalen and in Williams's tiny
office at Amen House. Neither Mr. Dyson nor my brother,
Major W. H. Lewis, will forget a certain immortal lunch at
Shirreff's in 1938 (he gave me a copy of *He Came Down From
Heaven* and we ate kidneys 'enclosed', like the wicked man, 'in
their own fat') nor the almost Platonic discussion which
followed for about two hours in St. Paul's churchyard. But in
1939 the Oxford University Press, and he with it, was evacuated
to Oxford. From that time until his death we met one another
about twice a week, sometimes more: nearly always on Thurs-

day evenings in my rooms and on Tuesday mornings in the
best of all public-houses for draught cider, whose name it would
be madness to reveal. The removal to Oxford also produced
other changes. The English Faculty was depleted by war and
Williams was soon making an Oxford reputation both as a
lecturer and as a private tutor. He became an honorary M.A.
It grew continually harder to remember that he had not always
been at Oxford. I am afraid that in our pride we half-imagined
that we must be the friends whom he had been in search of all
his life. Only since his death have we fully realized what a
small and late addition we were to the company of those who
loved him, and whom he loved.

In appearance he was tall, slim, and straight as a boy,
though grey-haired. His face we thought ugly: I am not sure
that the word 'monkey' has not been murmured in this context.
But the moment he spoke it became, as was also said, like the
face of an angel—not a feminine angel in the debased tradition
of some religious art, but a masculine angel, a spirit burning
with intelligence and charity. He was nervous (not shy) to
judge by the trembling of his fingers. One of the most characteristic things about him was his walk. I have often, from
the top of a bus, seen him walking below me. The face and
hair being then invisible, he might have passed for a boy in the
early twenties, and perhaps a boy of some period when swords
were worn. There was something of recklessness, something
even of *panache*, in his gait. He did not in the least swagger: but
if a clumsier man, like myself, had tried to imitate it a swagger
would probably have been the result. To complete the picture
you must add a little bundle under his left arm which was quite
invariable. It usually consisted of a few proofs with a copy of
Time and Tide folded round them. He always carried his head
in the air. When he lectured, wearing his gown, his presence
was one of the stateliest I have ever seen.

No man whom I have known was at the same time less
affected and more flamboyant in his manners: and also more
playful. The thing is very difficult to describe, partly because it
is so seldom seen. Perhaps it will be best imagined if I track it
to its sources, which were two. Firstly, he was a man fitted by
temperament to live in an age of more elaborate courtesy than
our own. He was nothing if not a ritualist. Had modern society
permitted it he would equally have enjoyed kneeling and being

knelt to, kissing hands and extending his hand to be kissed. Burke's 'unbought grace of life' was in him. But secondly, even while enjoying such high pomps, he would have been aware of them as a game: not a silly game, to be laid aside in private, but a glorious game, well worth the playing. This two-edged attitude, banked down under the deliberate casualness of the modern fashion, produced his actual manners, which were liked by most, extremely disliked by a few. The highest compliment I ever heard paid to them was by a nun. She said that Mr. Williams's manners implied a complete *offer* of intimacy without the slightest *imposition* of intimacy. He threw down all his own barriers without even implying that you should lower yours.

But here one of my collaborators breaks in upon me to say that this is not, after all, the true picture; that he, for his part, always found Williams a reserved man, one in whom, after years of friendship, there remained something elusive and incalculable. And that also seems to be true, though I doubt whether 'reserved' is the right name for it. I said before that he gave to every circle the whole man: all his attention, knowledge, courtesy, charity, were placed at your disposal. It was a natural result of this that you did not find out much about *him* —certainly not about those parts of him which your own needs or interests did not call into play. A selfless character, perhaps, always has this mysteriousness: and much more so when it is that of a man of genius.

This total offer of himself, but without that tacit claim which so often accompanies such offers, made his friendship the least exacting in the world, and explains the surprising width of his contacts. One kept on discovering that the most unlikely people loved him as well as we did. He was extremely attractive to young women and (what is rare) none of his male friends ever wondered why: nor did it ever do a young woman anything but immense good to be attracted by Charles Williams. Yet, on the other hand, all my memories of him are in bachelor surroundings where he was so at home—and to us speedily so indispensable—that you might have thought them the only surroundings he knew. That face—angel's or monkey's—comes back to me most often seen through clouds of tobacco smoke and above a pint mug, distorted into helpless laughter at some innocently broad buffoonery or eagerly stretched forward in the cut and parry of prolonged, fierce, masculine argument and 'the rigour of the game'.

Such society, unless all its members happen to be of one trade, makes heavy demands on a man's versatility. And we were by no means of one trade. The talk might turn in almost any direction, and certainly skipped 'from grave to gay, from lively to severe': but wherever it went, Williams was ready for it. He seemed to have no 'pet subject'. Though he talked copiously one never felt that he had dominated the evening. Nor did one easily remember particular 'good things' that he had said: the importance of his presence was, indeed, chiefly made clear by the gap which was left on the rare occasions when he did not turn up. It then became clear that some principle of liveliness and cohesion had been withdrawn from the whole party: lacking him, we did not completely possess one another. He was (in the Coleridgian language) an 'esemplastic' force. He was also, though not a professional scholar, one of the best informed of us all and will always stand in my mind as a cheering proof of how far a man can go with few languages and imperfect schooling. On the ancients and on the early Middle Ages there were one or two present with whom he could not compete, nor had he an exact knowledge of any of the great philosophers: but in history, theology, legend, comparative religion, and (above all) English literature from Shakespeare down, his knowledge was surprising. Malory, Shakespeare, Milton, Johnson, Scott, Wordsworth, Tennyson, Patmore, and Chesterton he seemed to have at his fingers' ends. Before he came I had passed for our best conduit of quotations: but he easily outstripped me. He delighted to repeat favourite passages, and nearly always both his voice and the context got something new out of them. He excelled at showing you the little grain of truth or felicity in some passage generally quoted for ridicule, while at the same time he fully enjoyed the absurdity: or, contrariwise, at detecting the little falsity or dash of silliness in a passage which you, and he also, admired. He was both a 'debunker' and (if I may coin the word) a 'rebunker'. *Fidelia vulnera amantis.*

This double-sidedness was the most strongly developed character of his mind. He might have appropriated Kipling's thanks

> to Allah who gave me two
> separate sides to my head,

except that he would have had to omit the word *separate*. The duality was much subtler than Kipling's, who in that poem really (I am afraid) intends little more than a repetition of Montaigne's *Que sçais-je?* In Williams the two sides lived in a perpetual dance or lovers' quarrel of mutual mockery. In most minds, and in his, the lower mocks at the higher; but in his the higher also mocked at the lower.

Thus on the one hand there lived in Williams a sceptic and even a pessimist. No man—and least of all the common run of antitheists—could have written a better attack on Christianity than he. He used to say that if he were rich enough to build a church he would dedicate it to St. Thomas Didymus Sceptic. He toyed with the idea that he and I should collaborate in a book of animal stories from the Bible, told by the animals concerned—the story of Jonah told by the whale or that of Elisha told by the two she-bears. The bears were to be convinced that God exists and is good by their sudden meal of children. He maintained that the prayer in which we give thanks 'for our creation' could be joined in only by an act of wholly supernatural faith. 'Thanks!' he would say, and then followed an eloquent pause. He was ready to accept as a revealed doctrine the proposition that existence is good: but added that it would never have occurred to him, unaided, to suspect this. He vehemently denied that he had any natural desire for life after death. In one of his earlier poems the man who is made ruler of three cities says

> I bore the labour, Lord,
> But cannot stomach the reward.

He even said, mocking himself while he said it, that if he were saved, the acceptance of eternal life would be not so much the guerdon as the final act of obedience. He also said that when young people came to us with their troubles and discontents, the worst thing we could do was to tell them that they were not so unhappy as they thought. Our reply ought rather to begin, 'But *of course*. . . .' For young people usually are unhappy, and the plain truth is often the greatest relief we can give them. The world is painful in any case: but it is quite unbearable if everyone gives us the idea that we are meant to be liking it. Half the trouble is over when that monstrous demand is withdrawn. What is unforgivable if judged as an hotel may be very tolerable as a reformatory. It is one of the many paradoxes in Wiiliams that while no man's conversation was less gloomy in *tone*—it was, indeed, a continual flow of gaiety, enthusiasm, and high spirits—no man at times said darker things. He never forgot the infinite menaces of life, the unremitted possibility of torture, maiming, madness, bereavement, and (over all) that economic insecurity which, as he said in *War in Heaven*, poisons our sorrows as well as modifying our joys.

But that was only one side of him. This scepticism and pessimism were the expression of his feelings. High above them, overarching them like a sky, were the things he believed, and they were wholly optimistic. They did not negate the feelings: they mocked them. To the Williams who had accepted the fruition of Deity itself as the true goal of man, and who deeply believed that the sufferings of this present time were as nothing in comparison, the other Williams, the Williams who wished to be annihilated, who would rather not have been born, was in the last resort a comic figure. He did not struggle to crush it as many religious people would have done. He saw its point of view. All that it said was, on a certain level, so very reasonable. He did not believe that God Himself wanted that frightened, indignant, and voluble creature to be annihilated; or even silenced. If it wanted to carry its hot complaints to the very Throne, even that, he felt, would be a permitted absurdity. For was not that very much what Job had done? It was true, Williams added, that the Divine answer had taken the surprising form of inviting Job to study the hippopotamus and the crocodile. But Job's impatience had been approved. His apparent blasphemies had been accepted. The weight of the divine displeasure had been reserved for the 'comforters', the self-appointed advocates on God's side, the people who tried to show that all was well—'the sort of people', he said, immeasurably dropping his lower jaw and fixing me with his eyes—'the sort of people who wrote books on the Problem of Pain'.

I have heard (from a lady) that he himself, before he went into hospital, had some expectation that he was going there to die. We, his male friends at Oxford, had had no notion that he was even ill until we heard that he was in the Radcliffe Infirmary; nor did we then suspect that the trouble was serious. I heard of his death at the Infirmary itself, having walked up there with a book I wanted to lend him, expecting this news that day as little (almost) as I expected to die that day myself. It was a Tuesday morning, one of our times of meeting. I thought he would have given me messages to take on to the others. When I joined them with my actual message—it was only a few minutes' walk from the Infirmary but, I remember, the very streets looked different—I had some difficulty in making them believe or even understand what had happened. The world seemed to us at that moment primarily a *strange* one.

That sense of strangeness continued with a force which sorrow itself has never quite swallowed up. This experience of loss (the greatest I have yet known) was wholly unlike what I should have expected. We now verified for ourselves what so many bereaved people have reported; the ubiquitous presence of a dead man, as if he had ceased to meet us in particular places in order to meet us everywhere. It is not in the least like a haunting. It is not in the least like the bitter-sweet experiences of memory. It is vital and bracing; it is even, however the word may be misunderstood and derided, exciting. A lady, writing to me after his death, used the word *stupor* (in its Latin sense) to describe the feeling which Williams had produced on a certain circle in London; it would almost describe the feeling he produced on us after he had died. There is, I dare say, no empirical proof that such an experience is more than subjective. But for those who accept on other grounds the Christian faith, I suggest that it is best understood in the light of some words that one of his friends said to me as we sat in Addison's Walk just after the funeral. 'Our Lord told the disciples it was expedient for them that He should go away for otherwise the Comforter would not come to them. I do not think it blasphemous to suppose that what was true archetypally, and in eminence, of His death may, in the appropriate degree, be true of the deaths of all His followers.'

So, at any rate, many of us felt it to be. No event has so corroborated my faith in the next world as Williams did simply by dying. When the idea of death and the idea of Williams thus met in my mind, it was the idea of death that was changed.

He was buried in St. Cross churchyard, where lie also the bodies of Kenneth Grahame and of P. V. M. Benecke.

C. S. L.

CONTENTS

'... AND TELLING YOU A STORY'

A NOTE ON *THE DIVINE COMEDY*

DOROTHY L. SAYERS

'I⊤ isn't at all what I expected,' said the friend whom I had persuaded into having a go at *The Divine Comedy*; 'I thought it would be all grand and solemn—you know—"Of Man's First Disobedience and the Fruit of that Forbidden Tree . . . Sing, Heavenly Muse," that sort of thing. But it's like someone sitting there in an arm-chair and telling you a story.'

My friend meant no disparagement to Milton, for whom she has an especial reverence. She meant only that since, somehow or other, nobody had ever taken the trouble to tell her what kind of poet Dante was, she had dimly supposed him to have written his great religious poem in the Miltonic, or the classical, or at any rate the 'epic' manner, and was astonished to find it start off with no more fuss than *The Pilgrim's Progress*, and so continue. My own experience was exactly the same as hers.

While I still knew Dante chiefly by his repute, *The Figure of Beatrice* was published, and I read it—not because it was about Dante, but because it was by Charles Williams. It became immediately evident that here was an Image, and here an Image-maker, with whom one had to reckon, and that the world had been right to call Dante a Great Poet—perhaps the greatest. But it was still some time before I made up my mind to tackle Dante in person; after all, fourteen thousand lines are fourteen thousand lines, especially if they are full of Guelfs and Ghibellines and Thomas Aquinas. A friendly critic can often give the impression that a poem is more colourful and exciting than it really is by picking out the jolly bits and passing over the rest, and I knew well enough the rambling and disjointed habits of the average medieval writer. Besides, the world always hinted that Dante, besides being great, grim, religious, and intellectual, was also 'obscure'. It was only a sense of shame and a series of accidents that made me at last blow off the dust from the three volumes of the Temple *Divine Comedy* which had originally belonged, I think, to my grandmother, and sit down to *Inferno*, Canto I, resolute, but inwardly convinced that I should read perhaps ten cantos with conscientious and self-conscious interest and attention, and then—in the way these things happen—one day forget to go on.

It did not happen that way. Coming to him as I did, for the first time, rather late in life, the impact of Dante upon my unprepared mind was not in the least what I had expected, and I can remember nothing like it since I first read *The Three Musketeers* at the age of thirteen. Neither the world, nor the theologians, nor even Charles Williams had told me the one great, obvious, glaring fact about Dante Alighieri of Florence —that he was simply the most incomparable story-teller who ever set pen to paper. However foolish it may sound, the plain fact is that I bolted my meals, neglected my sleep, work, and correspondence, drove my friends crazy, and paid only a distracted attention to the doodle-bugs which happened to be infesting the neighbourhood at the time, until I had panted my way through the Three Realms of the Dead from top to bottom and from bottom to top; and that, having finished, I found the rest of the world's literature so lacking in pep and incident that I pushed it all peevishly aside and started out from the Dark Wood all over again. In the course of these feverish wanderings I discovered three other things about Dante: first, that his diction was not, as I had imagined, uniformly in the grand manner, but homely, lucid, and fluent; secondly, that he himself was not, as tradition painted him, grim and austere, but sweet and companionable, and, if an archangel in stature, a very 'affable archangel'; thirdly, that he was a very great comic writer—which was quite the last thing one would ever have inferred from the things people say in their books.

When I say that Dante is a miraculous story-teller, I mean that he enthralled me with his story-telling; I have not bothered to find out who taught him to tell stories or where he got his stories from. He says Virgil taught him—and I can see for myself that he has, for example, taken a number of ideas from the sixth book of the *Aeneid* and distributed them judiciously in the places where they would do most good. I am aware that he read Ovid and Statius, and a mixed collection of philosophers from Aristotle to Aquinas, and that he knew the Vulgate inside out. But all that is of secondary importance; many people are steeped in Virgil, sodden with Aristotle, or Bible-ridden to the verge of mania, who yet cannot tell an after-dinner story without mislaying the point and making their audience 'yawn as

though overcome by fever or sleep'. Nor am I equipped to offer
any theories about the Veltro, or to expound the numerology of
the DXV, and the date of the *De Vulgari Eloquentia*, or to argue
about texts; very likely I shall come to that kind of thing in time,
but not now. At the moment I am only concerned with the
little gentleman, suitably (but not expensively) dressed, rather
stooping in the shoulders and tired about the eyes, who is at
present sitting in that arm-chair 'and telling you a story'.

'It consists', says J. W. Mackail of Thomson's unfortunate
poem on *Liberty*, 'of between three and four thousand lines of
blank verse, in the mixture of history, philosophy, politics and
preaching on which poets always make shipwreck when they
fail to fuse disparate and impracticable material by the heat of
poetical genius.' The *Divine Comedy* is all those things (except,
of course, that it is 14,000 lines long and in rhyme); it is also
a satire, a love-romance, a spiritual autobiography, and a story
of adventure. Because it is the last of these things it can afford
to be all the others. It has, to be sure, the heat of poetical
genius, without which 'all other words are but as dead cinders',
but though Dante rated his own genius at least as high as his
most fervent admirer has ever done, he had too good a sense of
reality to think he could do without the story. He had tried
already to improve people's minds by condescending to expound his Odes to them, expatiating on the pleasures of philosophy and, incidentally, upon his own impeccable behaviour
which had, he complained, been much misunderstood. But he
abandoned the attempt—possibly because his readers did not
seem to be responding, possibly because he realized that some of
the Odes were such that no ingenuity could represent them as
Hymns to Philosophy and get away with it—but chiefly, I think,
because during that period he had himself been down to Hell
and come up again, to be faced with himself at the top of Mount
Purgatory. It seems to me useless to ask what sin 'exactly' it
was which led to those sharp reproaches and those miserable
tears—whether it was a *pargoletta* or a theological error or a loss
of faith. One has only to compare the Dante of the *Convivio* with
the Dante of the *Vita* and the *Commedia* to see what it was that
had happened to him and then unhappened. The Dante of the
Convivio has everything that the other Dante has—the great
intellect, the great curiosity, the great poetry, the great piety,
even—but without humility and without charity. The sin is

not primarily girls or anybody's system of philosophy; it is simply the thing known as hardness of heart; and to recognize it there is no need to take a magnifying glass to the text to hunt out heresies, nor yet to pore over contemporary scandal to identify the lady of the Pietra poems. It is there, writ large—not 'a' sin, but simply sin. It was beginning to undermine his integrity when he 'came to himself' and found he was in the Dark Wood. And eventually he got out, or was led out (that is the story he is going to tell) and the frost in his heart broke up:

> lo gel che m' era intorno al cor ristretto,
> spirito ed acqua fessi.

(The ice that cramped me about the heart melted into breath and water.)

He stopped justifying himself and admitted that he was a fool and a miserable sinner. He took down the defensive barrier with which he had shut the 'blessed and glorious Beatrice' out of the *Convivio*. He stopped telling people how much older and mature he was than the Dante of the *Vita*, and accepted that dreaming, enthusiastic, gawky, and slightly absurd young man as his inalienable self. And he stopped lecturing people; and, throwing to the winds all his theories about noble diction and the elegant construction of Odes, he sat down, using any language that came handy—dialect forms, baby-language, Latin tags, nonsense-words, and even (if absolutely necessary) inferior lines of no more than ten syllables—and with colossal humility, colossal self-confidence, and a very practical charity he started telling them a story.

Not, of course, that the mere fact of telling a story was such proof of humility as it would have been had he lived 600 years later. He did, after all, call Virgil his 'master and author'; and nobody had taught him the strange theory of the early twentieth-century novelists, that one is a better story-teller for having no story to tell. He had not been, however, altogether free from the notion that talking over people's heads was a sign of superiority:

> Canzone, i' credo che saranno radi
> Color che tua ragione intendan bene,
> Tanto la parti faticosa e forte . . .

(Song, I think they will be few indeed that shall rightly understand thy meaning, so dark and intricate is thy utterance . . .)

and all the rest of it; and his manner towards his readers in the *Convivio*, though doubtless meant for their good, is often of the kind that would be 'intolerable from almighty God to a black-beetle'. In the *Comedy* there is a change of relationship: the reader is his familiar friend, entering into the story and entering sympathetically into his worst and weakest moments—'pensa, lettor, se io mi sconfortai'—'just think, reader, what a shock this gave me'; he is not trying to be obscure—those with sane intellects will divine the doctrine beneath the 'strange verses', or pierce the thin veil of the allegory; he is trying to be clear, and if his 'penna abborra'—if his pen runs astray—he begs to be excused—the subject is new and strange, or so lofty that he and every artist must fail. True, light-minded readers are advised not to follow him into the uncharted spaces of deep Heaven lest they should lose him and destroy themselves, but those who have fed on the Bread of Angels are welcome companions; and if, while our 'little skiffs' are trailing after him—as all the gondolas will collect in Venice behind a barge on which someone is singing, winding like a charmed serpent through canal after canal by moonlight—if, I say, he has suddenly the assurance to look round over his shoulder and catch us with our ears wagging and our eyes standing out like organ-stops:

> Pensa, lettor, se quel che qui s'inizia
> non procedesse, come tu avresti
> di più sapere angosciosa carizia,

(Think, reader, if I were to stop short in what I have begun, what an agony of suspense you would be in to know the rest)

the grin is a friendly one, and, dash it! he is perfectly right.

With a colossal humility, then, but with a colossal self-confidence all the same. Nobody who did not know beforehand what the *Comedy* was all about would guess from its opening the audacity of its scope and aim. Mr. C. S. Lewis has well pointed out the reason for the 'ritualistic or incantatory' style of the Virgilian and Miltonic epic. The invocation, the formal opening, the 'grand manner' are all there 'to give us the sensation that some great thing is now to begin', 'to compensate for—to counteract—the privacy and informality of silent reading in a man's own study'. That is true, and the *solempne* way is one great and right way with a great subject. Dante's way is not necessarily greater or more right; it is simply quite different. If

Boccaccio is telling the truth he did at one time intend to lose himself in an *O Altitudo*, and start off in the Latin tongue and the formal style:

> Ultima regna canam, fluido contermina mundo—

but all that unhappened with the rest of the great unhappening. By the time he has humbled himself to write in the vulgar tongue, 'in qua et mulierculae communicant', he is so certain of his vocation and his skill that he abandons, or at least post-pones, all ritual aids. He does not assume his singing robes; he merely assumes that he has them on, and he moves as freely in them as a practised actor in a period costume. He does not attempt to prepare the reader's mind; he merely walks casually into it and makes himself at home there. He does not try to counteract the informality of private reading; he takes advan-tage of it. Oddly enough, almost the first epithet which comes into one's mind for the style of the *Comedy* is 'unpretentious'. The poem does not start off like an epic, but with the disarming simplicity of a ballad or a romance or a fairy-tale:

> It fell about the Martinmas
>   When the wind blows shrill and cold . . .

> King Arthur was at Caerlleon upon Usk; and
>   one day he sat in his chamber . . .

> Childe Rowland and his brothers twain
>   Were playing at the ball . . .

> Nel mezzo del cammin di nostra vita
>   mi ritrovai per una selva oscura,
>   che la diritta via era smarrita.

(At the middle point of our life's journey I came to myself again in a dark wood, where the right way was lost.)

Dante has acknowledged his debt to his classical masters; but there must be, I think, also an unacknowledged debt to the romance-writers of the northern tradition, whom, after all, he had read. They are apt to begin with this kind of abruptness; and what, indeed, is he telling but a *roman courtois* of the achieve-ment of a lady by means of one of those other-world journeys in which the *matière de Bretagne* abounds? Only that where they are moving farther and farther from their supernatural origins into favour and prettiness, or sensation, or at the best a rather

tentative morality and psychology, he is moving back to the
origins and taking all the rest with him. And also (which is
more to my immediate purpose) that where they are rambling
and diffuse, he is pregnant, articulated, and architectural.

The structure of the thing is in every way astonishing.
Assuming that a story-teller is going to attempt this remarkable
mixture of 'history, philosophy, politics, and preaching', satire,
romance, autobiography, and adventure, what kind of form
would one expect him, nowadays, to give it? The obvious
answer is, the most elastic form possible, capable of the utmost
variety, so as to accommodate all this 'disparate and impracticable material'; 'film technique'—or, at the very least, the
elbow-room afforded by the chronicle-novel or the *roman
picaresque*; a broad treatment, without too much finicking detail,
and, above all, freedom from any suggestion of sameness or
monotony.

What Dante in fact does is to take the whole thing and cramp
it, as though into a steel corset, into three sets of concentric and
similar rings—forty-four rings in all—and to lead us remorse-
lessly, never missing a turn or a step, down four-and-twenty
rings one after the other, in which people are suffering various
forms of trouble and pain; then up ten rings one after another,
in nine of which people are suffering various forms of trouble
and pain; and finally up ten more rings, in which (for a change)
people are enjoying slightly varied forms of an unvarying bliss.
It sounds like the surest recipe for an almost screaming boredom. He need not have done it like that: the ten circular
Heavens may have been imposed on him by Ptolemaic astronomy; the twenty-four circles of Hell and the ten ascents of
Purgatory he went out of his way to invent. He liked it like
that; he deliberately chose for his material the most rigid form
conceivable, because he was a superb story-teller and knew,
first, that you can hold disparate material much better together
if you box it in so that it can't fall out; secondly, that you can
hold people's attention more closely to the matter in hand if you
focus it resolutely on some undeviating purpose (which is one
reason why detective stories are popular and why everybody is
so much more virtuous and industrious in war than in peace);
finally, that if you want the reader not only to follow but to
accept and believe a tale of marvels, you can do it best by the
accumulation of precise and even prosaic detail.

He started well equipped. He had a tidy mind, that loved order and symmetry for their own sake, or perhaps fell in love with them at the same time that he fell in love with scholastic theology. And the years that led him into the Dark Wood had not been wholly wasted by any means. Just as beneath the lovely fluency of the *terza rima*, which with a heart-breaking simplicity will do anything he wants—pray, sing, weep, thunder, grit its teeth, clinch an epigram, or report easy conversation in the high-comedy style—there lies the long apprenticeship to the fixed forms: ballata, sonnet, sestina, canzone; so the almost maddening schematization of the *Convivio*, with its parallelisms, divisions and sub-divisions, orderly digressions and orderly returns to the main path, throwing editors into a frenzy of analytical diagrams and marginal alphabets, underlies the massive coherence of the *Comedy*; in which nothing is displaced, or forgotten, or disconnected, or allowed to ramble out of proportion; and in which 'ogni parte ad ogni parte splende—each part reflects the light to every other', so that the whole scheme, as outlined in *Inferno*, i, is carried out unfalteringly to *Paradiso*, xxxiii; so that a question first raised in Hell may be answered in Purgatory, or a brilliant effect in the Heaven of the Fixed Stars plotted and prepared in the Eighth Chasm of Malebolge. In ten years of writing and fourteen thousand lines of verse there are few improvisations and scarcely an inconsistency; there is no disproportion.

Exactness and proportion by themselves will not, of course, make a story. The mere facts that the poem consists of precisely one hundred cantos, divided with as much symmetry as the nature of that number permits into books of thirty-four, thirty-three, and thirty-three cantos respectively; that between the longest and the shortest canto there is a difference of no more than forty lines; that each of the three Kingdoms of the Dead contains ten main divisions; that in the *Inferno* (which is the most complicated) the passage from Upper to Nether Hell comes almost exactly a quarter-way through the book, the passage from Violence to Fraud precisely half-way through, and the famous burlesque relief of the Ciampolo episode precisely half-way down Malebolge—these things may entertain the curious technician, but do not afford pleasure to the reader on first acquaintance, especially since they are so neatly managed that he probably will not notice them. But they do afford proof

to people who require proof of such things, that shapes do not
sculpture themselves, that oases of variety and refreshment do
not grow of their own accord in the arid soil of Hell, but are
put there, deliberately, at the points where they are calculated
to be most useful. It is just because order is so accurately observed that episodes and descriptions and similes and fragments
of Florentine politics and prophecies and prayers and humours
and grotesques can flourish so abundantly at every turn without
developing into jungly growths, obscuring the lines of the
structure, and holding up the pace of the narrative.

The sheer pace is, in fact, extraordinary. We start without
preliminary, and the first three lines inform us: that the story is
to describe the poet's own experience; it is to be told in the first
person; he is thirty-five years old; it is a story about a journey,
and has an allegorical meaning connected with 'the Way'—
the *cammin di nostra vita*; the traveller has come to himself after
some sort of aberration and has found that he is in a Dark Wood,
and has lost his way. At the thirteenth line we come to the
Mountain, and are thus linked immediately to the subject of
the second book; at line thirty-one the Leopard arrives, followed
within twenty lines by the Lion and the She-Wolf, thus preparing
us for the three main divisions of Hell. After another dozen lines
Virgil appears, and there is a pause while he establishes himself
and Dante gives us a rapid sketch of his own poetic derivation.
Then come nine lines of prophecy about the Veltro, hinting at
an eschatological significance, and at the same time laying
stress on the whole allegory of 'the City'; after that the entire
scope and subject of the three books is mapped out, and the
journey is begun. One could scarcely get more work out of a
hundred and thirty-five lines. And indeed, lest the pace should
become so quick as to appear casual, Canto II checks it abruptly.
(Here an invocation at last makes its appearance. It is addressed
to the Muse, Genius and Memory, and occupies exactly three
lines.) Dante baulks—as we shall see him do a good many
times, up to that last, pathetic, poignant, and most piercingly
comic baulk of all on the Cornice of Fire—and produces a whole
set of highly cogent and perfectly ridiculous reasons for not
going on. The reasons are ridiculous, because he has, in fact,
no choice but either to go on or remain for ever in the Dark
Wood which is more terrible than death, but our heart warms
to his absurdity: his excuses are so like the excuses we make for

ourselves. Virgil's reply introduces Beatrice, sums up in a line or two everything which the reader needs to know (if he has not previously read the *Vita*) about the previous Dante–Beatrice connexion, and lays down the lines on which the *Paradiso* is to develop. Incidentally we get to know a good deal more about Virgil himself: the three chief figures of the *Comedy* are established. The action has paused, but the story has advanced. The two poets—surely the most charming couple that ever walked side by side through a story—set off again; and then, suddenly, at the opening of the Third Canto, we are really there. For the first time the authentic Grand Manner makes its appearance, and the verse rings like iron:

> Per me si va nella città dolente;
> per me si va . . .

(Through me the road goes to the sorrowful city; through me . . .)

and through the gate we go, abandoning everything. Nothing could now keep us from the adventure.

It is a story of adventure. And it is written as all the best adventure stories are written. From century to century the trick is rediscovered—by Defoe, by Bunyan, by Jules Verne, by Conan Doyle, by H. G. Wells—and new generations thrill with astonished delight. The titles of three of Jules Verne's tales might well serve as sub-titles for the three books of the *Comedy*: *Voyage au Centre de la Terre*; *L'Île Mystérieuse*; *De la Terre à la Lune*—except that the last is not quite adventurous enough. And the trick is always the same trick: it is the trick—and to some minds the scandal—of particularity. Some very great poets have preferred to tell their stories without it, and done well; some great story-tellers who were not poets at all have used it and have also done well. When it is used by a story-teller who is also a poet of Dante's calibre the effect is extra-ordinary. Two kinds of excitement are blended together to make an excitement less heady than the excitement of either poetry or story-telling by itself, but more thirst-quenching than either. What the trick of particularity adds to the poetry is, I think, best described as a vivid conviction of fact—the sort of conviction that used to lead people to address letters to 'Sherlock Holmes Esq., 221 Baker Street', begging him to investigate their problems. We believe in Dante's Three Kingdoms; not as we believe in the magic landscapes of Spenser or Keats, or

even of Milton (though he had a touch of the trick too)—that is,
by a willing surrender of the judgement to the spell-binding
power of beautiful or terrible words. We believe in the Inferno
as we believe in Robinson Crusoe's island—because we have
trudged on our own two feet from end to end of it. We are
convinced that it is *there*, independently of the poet; if necessary,
we could find our way through it without him. We know the
landmarks and should recognize them, just as we should recognize Crusoe's cave, or his arbour, or the place where the miraculous crop of wheat came up, or the current that threatened
to carry him and his boat out to sea. It is not merely that, as
Macaulay has pointed out,[1] Dante, having claimed to be the
eye-witness and ear-witness of that which he relates, is obliged
to substantiate his claim by minute particulars. 'The reader
would throw aside such a tale in incredulous disgust, unless it
were told with the strongest air of veracity, with a sobriety even
in its horrors, with the greatest precision and multiplicity in its
details.' That is true; it is true also that 'he is the very man who
has heard the tormented spirits crying out for the second death,
who has read the dusky characters on the portal within which
there is no hope, who has hidden his face from the terrors of the
Gorgon, who has fled from the hooks and the seething pitch of
Barbariccia and Draghinazzo.' But that is not all; the important thing is that *we* have been there, and can indeed scarcely
free ourselves from a dreadful conviction that one day we might
even *go* there. The road is more clearly mapped even than that
other road, 'straight as a rule can make it', that runs from the
Wicket Gate to the Celestial City; we know every outline by
sight and every variation in the murky light: the serene illumination of the Elysian Fields, the red glow of the iron walls of Dis,
the fiery rain, the moving flames 'like fireflies' in the Eighth
Bolgia, the pale glimmer of the ice at the bottom of the Pit. If
we were led through Hell blindfold, the familiar sounds would
tell us where we were: the sighs and wailings, and the wuther-
ing of the *bufera infernal*, the howls of Cerberus, the yells of
the hoarders and spendthrifts, the splashing and bubbling of
the streams, the shrieks of the Furies, the sibilant voices of the
Suicides 'sizzling like green wood on the fire', the thunder of the
cataract, the snuffling and blowing of the Flatterers, the quar-
rels and shouts of the Malebranche, the confused roar of the

[1] *Essay on Milton.*

speaking flames, the teeth of the Traitors chattering like storks
—all the hideous, intolerable clamour of Hell. And if we were
both deaf and blind, we could almost smell our way through
from stink to stink.

Coming to the Baedeker-like precision of Dante from the rich
texture and vague vast suggestiveness of later poets, we may be
inclined to feel that he lacks 'poetry'. It is true that he has no
sustained passages of grandiose and sensuous description in
which the mind can, as it were, plunge and lose itself; you
could not, for example, pick out a hundred lines or so of terrible
grandeur to set beside Milton's picture of the journey through
Chaos. Such descriptive matter as there is is brief and austere
to starkness:

> Non fronde verdi, ma di color fosco;
>   non rami schietti, ma nodosi e involti;
>   non pomi v'eran, ma stecchi con tosco . . .

(No green there, but only dark, discoloured leaves; no smooth
boughs, but all twisted and gnarled; no fruit, but withered twigs
with poison . . .)

> Sopra tutto il sabbion d'un cader lento
> piovean di foco dilatate falde,
> come di neve in alpe senza vento . . .

(Slowly dropping over all the sand there drifted down huge flakes
of fire, as snow falls in the Alps on a windless day . . .)

A whole landscape of Perugino-like loveliness may be evoked
and dismissed in a line or two:

> Dolce color d'oriental zaffiro
> che s'accoglieva nel sereno aspetto
> dell' aer puro infino al primo giro . . .

(The tender hue of orient sapphire, gathering upon the tranquil
forehead of the sky, pure even to the first circle . . .)

> . . . di lontano
> conobbi il tremolar della marina . . .

(. . . from afar I recognized the shimmering of the sea, . . .).

But what is 'poetry'? By some it is taken to mean the removal
of concepts to a plane on which they become acceptable to the
emotions just because, at that level, they neither demand the
assent of the intellect nor challenge any issue in conduct. Thus

we may accept Hell (or the Incarnation of God, or the brother-hood of Man or what not) 'in a poetic sense' without feeling the need to do anything about it. To Dante this kind of poetry would have seemed (if nothing worse)

> a barren noise[1]
> Though it blows legend-laden through the trees.

He conceives that 'his whole business is to show us Hell', and that is precisely what he shows us—not 'the poetry of Hell', but simply Hell. Although he may, and I think does, make it acceptable to the intellect, to the complacent emotions Dante's Hell is not acceptable, nor does he mean it to be. He desires that his Hell should evoke an emotional repulsion, issuing in a vigorous rejection by the will, just as he desires that his Purgatory and Paradise should be embraced, with equal vigour, by the undivided personality. If by 'poetry' we mean some sort of 'backward mutters of dissevering power' which can dis-join the imagination from the will, then Dante is the least poetical of poets.

But if poetry has anything to do with compelling the imagina-tion itself, then Dante's grand art does not fail him. We may think that he works by statement rather than by suggestion: yet in the end we find that he has suggested more than the content of his statements. Their effect is cumulative. As we are led down, relentlessly, from circle to circle of Hell, the steady piling-up of dry detail—the noise, stench, and squalor, the grit and greyness, the sterility, stuffiness, and heat, the narrowing circles, the weight and pressure of tier upon tier of rock, the sense of everything shelving down and closing in, ends by producing an oppression of spirits and an increasing claustro-phobia compared with which a trip through Milton's Hell is as refreshing as an open-air picnic. Even in damnation, Mil-ton's devils can *do* something—dig for metals, build a palace, make a causeway over Chaos; but here there is only an incessant restlessness without change, a monotonous miserable activity to no purpose, the fixation of choice, the endless self-devouring of the will turned in upon itself. The place is evil, with an evil stripped of its last shred of glitter; and the deeper we go the more suffocating does the atmosphere become, and the meaner grows the aspect of the evil selfhood thus stripped naked. 'It is

[1] Keats, *Fall of Hyperion*.

extraordinary,' said the friend I have already quoted, on arriv-
ing at the bottom of the Tenth Bolgia; 'when you look back from
here, the upper part of Hell seems almost gay by comparison,
with its rivers and cities and picturesque monsters.' The dis-
appearance of ornament has much to do with this, by negative
suggestion; and so also has the mere looking back—the looking
up the four thousand miles of that colossal shaft. From the ice
of Cocytus Dante looks up, as in the *Paradiso* he will look down
over the seven spheres and see the earth:

> tal ch'io sorrisi del suo vil sembiante—
> (such that I smiled at its sorry appearance).

'Look down', says Beatrice, 'and see how great a universe I
have put under thy feet.' So, in the *Inferno*, a world is piled
over his head. Its enormity is measured by the measure of our
relief when we emerge 'to look once more upon the stars'—the
stars from which we shall presently see that same enormity
dwindled to a pin's-head insignificance.

Continually, indeed, Dante's poetry suggests more than its
statements contain. Once, having spoken enthusiastically of
the exquisite colour in which the Ante-Purgatorio was bathed,
I referred to the text for corroboration, and in all eight cantos
could discover only a dozen lines which mentioned colour at
all—the rest was pure suggestion and the poet's magic. However, the poetry of Dante is not our business at the moment.
What concerns us is that the spell-binding which we choose to
call 'the poetry' as distinct from the poem is always so controlled that it cannot hypnotize us into losing contact with story
and meaning.

This, for a long narrative poem, is of enormous importance.
Our inability to resist being carried unobservantly away on long
rollers of sensuous rhythm is the reason why Swinburne's *Tristram* fails to hold us as a narrative. And I think that a kind of
spell-bound submission to the sheer dignity of the Miltonic line
accounts largely for our tendency to accept Milton's Satan at
his own valuation. For a moment the ugly 'squat like a toad'
shocks us into noticing what it is that we are so ready to admire.
But when it comes to Hell, then, however often we meet with
words denoting pain and horror and degradation, the style
itself is too much for us; 'the grand, infernal peers' remain—
we cannot help it—grand. Even the horrible allegory of Sin

and Death nowhere touches the squalid depth of grotesque and
impotent misery that affronts us in:

> con sei occhi piangeva, e per tre menti
> gocciava il pianto e sanguinosa bava.

(He wept from his six eyes, and down his three chins ran tears and
bloody slaver.)

I know no poet who can compare with Dante in the 'art of
sinking'—and rising again—'in poetry'. Not even Shakespeare
can do it so swiftly and surely. The miracle of the style is its
fluidity—it moves like water, taking on every contour of the
great rock-sculptured mass over which it flows. Look, for
instance, at the delicious, almost drawing-room-comedy light-
ness of the little dialogue on the Fifth Cornice where the two
poets meet Statius, and Dante, by an inopportune smile, gives
away Virgil's identity. Statius's mild indignation at what looks
like bad manners, Virgil's humorous resignation, and Dante's
schoolboy confusion are sketched with the delicate accuracy
of the novel of manners—the trifling social *gaffe* might almost
be occurring to Miss Catherine Morland in the Pump Room
at Bath; and then, in a turn, in a twinkling, and without the
slightest jerk in the line, we are pulled back to the tremendous
scene and the cosmic realities: this is Mount Purgatory, these
are Statius and Virgil, and they are great and dead:

> Già si chinava ad abbracciar li piedi
> al mio dottor; ma egli disse: 'Frate,
> non far, chè tu se' ombra, ed ombra vedi.'

(Already he was stooping to embrace my Doctor's feet; but he
said to him: 'Brother, do not so; for shade you are and look upon a
shade.')

The story moves, and the style with it. Never, whether by
over-lightness or over-loading, by any 'inappropriate splendour', or by the *lussuria* of a too-prolonged lusciousness, does
the obedient 'poetry' betray its proper function.

Structure, speed, particularity, style—what next? Why, to
be sure, that quality without which a tale may indeed take
captive the imagination but can never root itself in the affec-
tions—the power to create a whole universe of breathing
characters. It is often a fatal weakness in allegory to be popu-
lated by droves of frigid abstractions and perambulating labels;
it is on his ability to endow these figures with the breath of life

that the allegorist depends for his enduring persuasiveness. In this art Bunyan is, I suppose, acknowledged master, and it would be a bold man who should maintain that even Dante equalled or surpassed him. What one can say is that Dante, by an inspired tact in choosing his subject, side-stepped this besetting difficulty of allegory. His fable is such that he can fill his poem with real people who do not cease to be their earthly selves because they also typify everybody's sins and virtues. Dante is guided through Hell and Purgatory, not by Conscience, or Wisdom, or Counsel, or Good-wit, or what-not, but by Virgil —a Virgil who is not merely utterly charming and human, after the manner of Faithful or Mr. Ready-to-Halt, but is also so personally Virgil that he cannot resist telling the story of the founding of Mantua, and that in quoting (and indeed mis-quoting) his own poem he observes negligently to Dante: 'My high Tragedy sings him somewhere or other—you'll remember, since you have the whole poem by heart.' 'Non uomo, uomo già fui'—he is not, but he was once a man—that is why his nostalgia can catch so terribly at one's heart:

> Vespero è già colà, dov' è sepolto
> lo corpo, dentro al quale io facea ombra:
> Napoli l' ha, e da Brandizio è tolto.

(It is already evening yonder, where lies the body in which I once cast a shadow; Naples has it now, and it was brought thither from Brindisi.)

That is why Sordello's anxious question is almost intolerably poignant:

> O pregio eterno del loco ond' io fui,
> qual merito o qual grazia mi ti mostra?
> S'io son d'udir le tue parole degno,
> dimmi se vien d'inferno, e di qual chiostra.

(O eternal glory of my birthplace, what merit or what grace grants me the sight of you? If I am worthy to hear you speak, tell me if you come from Hell, and from what cloister there.)

Immortal courtesy gives him what reassurance it can; immortal courtesy receives it without comment; the fact of immortal sundering and immortal loss stands desolately between them.

So too with the other souls: blessed or damned, they remain eternally themselves. Cacciaguida is not just Ancestry or De-rivation—he is that sturdy old Florentine gentleman, steeped in

the archives—one might almost say the gossip—of the city.
Belacqua, purging his laziness on the lower slopes of Purgatory,
is lazy Belacqua still, curled sleepily with his face between his
knees, and bestirring himself, to twit Dante, with the smallest
possible expenditure of energy:

> Allor si volse a noi, e pose mente,
> movendo il viso pur su per la coscia.

(Then he turned and looked at us consideringly, moving only his
face as it rested upon his thigh.)

As the damned become more and more dehumanized in the
fixed quality of their corruption the closer they lie to the bottom
of the Pit, so the survival of their essential personality becomes
more and more shocking to us. The human pathos and the
rippling beauty of Master Adam's agonizing vision of unattainable water:

> Li ruscelletti, che dei verdi colli
> del Casentin discendon giuso in Arno,
> facendo i lor canali freddi e molli,
> sempre mi stanno innanzi, e non indarno. . .

(The little brooks that from the green hills of the Casentin run
down into the Arno, making their channels cool and moist—these
haunt me for ever, and not for nothing. . .)

make still more hideous its resolution into an inhuman bestiality
of vindictiveness:

> Ma s'io vedessi qui l'anima trista
> di Guido o d'Alessandro o di lor frate,
> per fonte Branda non darei la vista.

(But if I could only see here the miserable soul of Guido or Alex-
ander or their brother, I would not miss that sight for all the water
in the fountain of Branda.)

Even the mythical monsters and 'greedy organisms of hell' are
not *just* embodied attributes. They were once something that
had to do with human life and poetry; Chiron is a person, and
indeed a sympathetic person—he and his centaurs gallop round
the shore of Phlegethon:

> come solean nel mondo andare a caccia.

(as in the world they used to go a-hunting.)

Cerberus is not simply a projection of gluttonous desire; he is
a dog, a classic dog and an old acquaintance, existing apart
from his allegorical function.

Charles Williams has memorably established for us the
reality of the figure of Beatrice herself;[1] and Dean Church has
summed up the matter in a pregnant sentence: 'We may infer
from the *Convito* that the eyes of Beatrice stand definitely for
the *demonstrations*, and her smiles for the *persuasions* of wisdom;
but the poetry of the *Paradiso* is not about demonstrations and
persuasions, but about looks and smiles.'[2] It is not sufficient
to allow that Beatrice is *a* real woman; she is *that* real woman:
the same Florentine girl who once made fun of Dante at a party,
who once cut him in the street, whose mere presence in the
same city with him filled him with inexplicable anguish and
ecstasy. In the *Purgatorio* the refusal of her salutation is more
shattering; in the *Paradiso* her laughter is a thing that he learns,
rapturously, to bear. The young man's unforgettable experience is taken up—repeated and resolved upon a higher level.
Strangely enough, he has not told us in the *Vita* how, or even
whether, the Florentine Beatrice forgave him and restored the
blessing of her *salute*; we shall now never know whether the
reconciliation with the celestial Beatrice is the image of something that did happen or only of something that might and
ought to have happened. Either way, the thing bears the stamp
of authenticity: two real lovers are estranged; they meet,
quarrel, and are reconciled; a new relationship is established.
The story is more than that, but it is at least that.

The greatness of the story-teller is seen in the handling of the
story. If Dante needed any model for his love-romance outside
his own experience he might—and indeed he may—have found
it in Chrestien de Troyes' *Charrette*. Here, too, the lover, after
a long and perilous series of adventures, wins through to the
presence of his lady. She receives him coldly and repudiates
him. The King pleads for Lancelot, rather as the attendant
Graces plead for Dante: 'Lady, why do you shame him so?'
At this point in the French romance there intervenes a debauch
of sentimentalities: Lancelot leaves the court, is captured and
reported killed; Guinevere becomes ill with remorse, and *she* is
reported dead; Lancelot hears the rumour and tries to commit
suicide; Guinevere again hears that he is dead and again falls
into a transport of grief. Eventually these misunderstandings
are cleared up and the lovers once more brought face to face;

---

[1] *The Figure of Beatrice*, from which I have quoted various phrases *passim*.
[2] *Essay on Dante.*

Guinevere reproaches Lancelot for having failed in that utter devotion exacted by the code of courtly love; tears of penitence are shed (in this case on both sides) and thereafter they are reconciled and Lancelot becomes Guinevere's lover within the meaning of the act.

Disregarding the comparative vulgarity of Chrestien's intrigue, the resemblance in structural outline between these two 'turning-point' episodes is sufficient to show at once the *Comedy*'s debt to the *roman courtois* and the distance it has travelled beyond it. The Beatrician element in the *Comedy* is simply the transvaluation of 'courtly love' to a plane on which it makes profound spiritual sense instead of social chaos. But, setting all this aside, what leaps to the eye is the enormous advance in technique by which Dante has made the characters their own destiny, and their actual confrontation in itself both the crisis and the resolution. Chrestien—an excellent story-teller of his kind—dissipates his situation in repeated efforts to pile up the agony, so that in the end the reconciliation, separated by so much time, space, and bustle from the repudiation-scene, falls curiously flat. Even so, the reconciliation is not itself the crisis: it merely prepares the real crisis of the poem. Dante, coming to his task a hundred years later, an incomparably greater poet with an incomparably greater story to tell, reveals in addition an incomparably greater power of sheer narration. He has the essential dramatic gift—an unerring sense of the *scène à faire*, and upon that scene he single-mindedly concentrates, dissipating no energy, welding action and character together with an intense economical compactness of passion and irony, until he has wrung the resolution of the situation out of the situation itself. It is the technique of the psychological novel, centuries in advance of its time, and it bears no marks of immaturity or fumbling. But the mind of Dante is so adult that it is always difficult to remember that he died twenty years before Chaucer was born, and forged his own language as he wrote it.

Which brings us to the figure of Dante himself. There have been many schools of thought about Beatrice, but nobody (so far) has attempted to disprove the actual existence of Dante. Like so many writers of adventure-stories, he has told his tale in the first person, and it is usually conceded that the adventure described is substantially his own, whether there is any element

of 'vision' in it or whether it is merely an imaginative record
of interior experience. The autobiographical method has two
enormous advantages for this kind of story-telling: it surrounds
the most startling occurrences with a powerful illusion of veri-
similitude, and it prevents the narrative from becoming disjointed and flying apart in all directions. Its danger is that the
adventuring ego will become either a self-glorifying bore or else
a characterless mirror for the reception of fleeting impressions.
Dante avoids both these pitfalls by a brilliant technical expedient for which he has never (I think) been given sufficient
credit. Except for those clearly indicated passages in which he
allows his prophetic function, and not himself, to speak by his
mouth, he has conceived his own character from start to finish
in a consistent spirit of comedy. Seldom has an autobiographer
presented the world with a less heroic picture 'of himself, or
presented his own absurdities so lovably. Whether he is mum-
bling excuses for himself in the Dark Wood, or turning green
in the face before the Gates of Dis, or lingering like a reluctant
child at Farinata's tomb while his escort is calling him to come
on, or being 'less intelligent than usual' about the *Ethics*, or
pottering 'bemused' along rocky terraces in imminent peril of
falling off, or likening himself to a little goat, or a baby stork,
or to a man walking along the street in blissful unconsciousness
of something funny stuck in his hat, or asking inappropriate
questions which make Beatrice look at him 'as a mother looks
on her delirious child', or trotting forward to answer St. Peter's
viva voce 'like a Baccalaureate, equipping himself with every
argument' and anxious to do credit to himself and his teachers,
his self-portrait is saturated with a delicate and disarming
awareness of himself as a comic figure. I do not think this is
just a craftsman's device—I think it is, on the contrary, a sincere
and touching humility. The fact remains that no other treatment of himself could have served his artistic ends so well. It
enables him to dissect himself with an almost alarming acute-
ness and candour; it imparts a singular balance and truthfulness
to his relationship with Virgil; it turns the plunge into the fire
of the Seventh Cornice from the conventional heroic gesture it
might so easily have been into the kind of exhibition which
leaves us uncertain whether to laugh or cry; it sharpens the edge
of that crucial humiliation on the banks of Lethe, and at the
same time makes it just tolerable—we feel it embarrassing and

almost indecent to see any human creature stripped so naked, and yet we accept it, since humiliation, one way and another, is the lot of every comic character.

His own is not, of course, the only comic character in Dante. There are the ugly, rollicking, Ingoldsby-Legend burlesques of the Fifth Bolgia, conceived in a mood of savage satire and tearing high spirits. There are sly satiric portraits like that of Belacqua. There are the preposterous Nimrod and the vain Antaeus; there is Pope Nicholas, grotesquely wedged upside-down and 'lamenting with his shanks' while Dante adds to the discomforts of Hell by chanting a solemn denunciation at him:

> forte spingava con ambo le piote
>
> (he jerked violently with both his feet)

no wonder! There are those charming shades in the Ante-Purgatorio who, having died excommunicate, wander out their waiting-time like shepherdless sheep:

> e ciò che fa la prima, e l'altre fanno,
>   addossandosi a lei s'ella s'arresta,
>   semplici e quete, e lo 'mperchè non sanno.

(And what the first one does the others do, bumping up against her when she stops, silly and meek, and not knowing why.)

There are, at every turn, lines and similes through which irrepressible little chuckles bubble up—images of squatting and darting frogs, sleepy ostlers, or sculptured corbels which give the beholder a crick in the back to look at them; shrewd little comments on human nature; polite ironies and friendly leg-pulls—together with turns of phrase so equivocal and delivered with such a poker-faced gravity that it is hard to be certain whether mockery is intended or not. Once there is the faintest flicker of a smile at Virgil—him, even—when he has allowed himself to be taken in by the Malebranche and is drily mocked for his credulity by Fra Catalano:

> Appresso il duca a gran passi sen gì
>   turbato un poco d'ira nel sembiante.

(At this my guide marched off with raking strides, looking upset and rather angry.)

'A gran passi'; there is pique in every line of that striding form.

Dante the pilgrim hastens on, distressed, 'following the prints of the beloved feet'; but as Dante the poet looks after them his mouth twitches, just perceptibly, at the corners.

But the comedy of the *Comedy* is matter for a small treatise in itself. I will only reaffirm my (possibly revolutionary) opinion that Dante Alighieri is a very great comic artist indeed, with a range extending from Swift on the one hand to Jane Austen on the other; and that his comic spirit is an enormous asset to his story-telling.

But the comic spirit, delighting as it does in disproportion and incongruity, is itself the best safeguard against these errors, and it is precisely this genius for comedy that endows Dante with the all-important gift of tact. I do not mean that he never gives offence to anybody; few writers have given so much to so many people, and no writer worth his salt gives none. I am thinking of the special brand of tact displayed by the ingenious traveller in Saki's tale appropriately entitled *The Story-Teller*. It consists largely in the avoidance of unnecessary difficulties and imprudently-placed explanations. It is a trick of narration which prevents the children from interrupting with questions at the wrong moment. I have mentioned Dante's choice of real people for the images of his allegory as an instance of this tact; he is thus enabled to make them exhibit a multiplicity of human traits and interests which would be unsuitable in *merely* allegorical figures—'accidents in a substance' and no more. 'Why' (one would begin to ask) 'should a simple personification of Dante's own evil passions pester him with inquiries about the present state of Romagna, or an emblematic figure of Repentance go out of its way to instruct him in embryology?' But given the right choice of fable to start with, there are still a number of things which have to be explained—it is indeed a great part of the intention of the poem that they should be explained; and the tactful placing of these explanations provides an absolute model of sheer narrative skill.

There has to be, for example, some sort of verbal map to explain the very complicated divisions and sub-divisions of Hell. But it would never do for Virgil, or the author, to hold us up at the beginning of the adventure with a lengthy disquisition on the *Ethics*. If he did, Dante might still have courage to embark on the journey, but the reader quite certainly would not. So we are led at a brisk pace through the Vestibule and

the first five Circles with little more than the necessary Cook's-
Tour commentary: 'On your left, Westminster Abbey; on your
right, the Houses of Parliament; the statues in the square are
those of distinguished statesmen; observe the pigeons; there is
Westminster Bridge, made famous in Wordsworth's sonnet; this
is the Thames Embankment.' Then follow two cantos of alarms
and excursions—the passage of Styx, the burning walls of Dis,
opposition by devils, the dread of losing Virgil, the slammed
gates, Furies, Gorgons, the tremendous apparition of the Angel
and the triumphant entry. Then, a little calmer in mind but
still excited, we interview Farinata in his burning tomb. So far
so good, and the story has carried us along by sheer impetus.
But the time has arrived when we really must know where we
are going and what it is all about, or we shall become puzzled
and fretful and keep on wondering why this and why that, when
we ought to be attending to the images. So a pause is made—
the poet can afford it, for we could no more get away from him
now than from the Ancient Mariner; and we are really glad of it,
for the pace has made us breathless, and we are quite content
to sit down behind the tomb of Anastasius and have a little
lesson in infernal geography and the various kinds of sins. The
timing is perfect: earlier, we should not have listened; later, we
should have had too much difficulty in remembering the ground
we have gone over. But now it can be done, all in one go, and
finished with, and not intruded upon us in places where it would
only distract us by interrupting the story.

    There are, however, other questions, of a specifically awkward
sort, which are bound to crop up eventually in any tale which
has to handle a mixture of spiritual and physical bodies. It is,
I think, pretty safe to say that nobody, reading the *Inferno* for
the first time with his mind on the story, was ever seriously
worried by any query about weights and measures, any more
than he would be in reading a fairy-tale. Dante is there in his
physical body; the shades are not—so much is insisted on and
we accept it. The innumerable anomalies with which the story
is packed do not trouble us. Hell is, apparently, a great funnel
stretching down to the centre of the physical globe, 'on which
all weights down-weigh', yet Dante in his physical body can
cover the 4,000 miles or so of the descent in thirty-six hours
without food or sleep. Very well, he can; in this nightmare
place anything can happen. The shades are *vanità*, yet Dante

can twist the hair of Bocca's head, and Virgil, 'weightless' as he is, has yet solidity enough to pick Dante up and carry him, as the spectral boat of Phlegyas can carry him. The boat's gun-wale sinks deep under the unaccustomed load; Virgil is exhausted by the scramble down and up the flanks of Dis; well and good—there is classic precedent for that kind of thing. Dante can cross the rivulet which moats the Elysian castle 'as though upon dry ground', but he cannot so cross Phlegethon, nor can Virgil carry him; they have to enlist the aid of a Centaur. Dante tells us these things and we do not question them because he takes it for granted that we shall not.

But the time is coming when such questions cannot be avoided, if only for the reason that it is part of Dante's intention to tell us about the nature of these spiritual- or rather, of these interim-bodies,'which at the Resurrection will be replaced by the true spiritual bodies, the 'glorious and holy flesh' in its final glory and sanctity. And being faced by this necessity, Dante grapples with it in the proper craftsman's way—he turns it to glorious gain. We have ended our nightmare groping through Hell; we are on the fresh and open shores at the foot of Mount Purgatory; the ship of blessed souls has touched land; the sun is rising and our spirits are rising with it. It is at this moment that Dante is dealt two sharp shocks in swift succession: he finds that the form of Casella has no substance and the form of Virgil casts no shadow. He is suddenly reminded of the otherness of those beloved souls. The moment of panic when he sees his own shadow thrown solitary upon the hillside recalls that earlier terror before the gates of Dis; it anticipates and prepares us for that silent final separation in the Earthly Paradise, for which 'all that our First Mother lost' can hardly console either Dante or us. But now look how skilfully the rising curiosity is diverted, half-satisfied, quelled, and transmuted into a wholly different emotion. 'Why do you distrust? Do you not believe that I am with you and guide you? The body in which I used to cast a shadow is the world's width away—as for this:

> A sofferir tormenti e caldi e gieli
>   simili corpi la virtù dispone,
>   che, come fa, non vuol che a noi si sveli.

(To suffer torment, heat and cold, bodies such as this are allotted by that Power which chooses not to unveil its workings to us.)

Reason cannot compass the infinite mysteries of the Godhead—
if it could

> 'mestier non era partorir Maria;
> e disiar vedeste senza frutto
>   tai, che sarebbe lor disio quetato,
>   ch'eternalmente è dato lor per lutto.
> Io dico d'Aristotele e di Plato
>   e di molti altri.' E qui chinò la fronte;
>   e più non disse, e rimase turbato.

('... there had been no need for Mary to conceive. And you have
seen great men desire in vain, whose desire might else have been
fulfilled—but now it is given to them for an eternal grief. I speak of
Aristotle and Plato, and of many others.' And here he bent his head
and said no more, and remained troubled.)

'And of many others.' Distress for Virgil's sake drives all other
feelings from our minds; inquisitiveness seems here an impertinence, and it is not till we have pulled ourselves together that we
realize that our question has in fact been answered. The bodies
'disposed' to the souls are sufficient for what is required of them;
they 'exist for the sake of their function and not their function
for them'. If, in the Divine intention, it is necessary that the
dead Virgil should be able to carry the living Dante, the strength
is supplied; if it is undesirable that Dante should embrace Casella, the substance is withdrawn. Subsequently, the mechanism (so to call it) of the airy body is explained by Statius, high
up on the Sixth Cornice, objectively, and in connexion with
spirits for whom it is possible to feel a more detached and less
emotional interest.

The skill and delicacy with which all this is done can best be
appreciated by observing how the same problem is handled by
Milton. Great and high and delicate poet as he is, Milton is
just lacking in Dante's faultless tact. Adam, courteously wel-
coming Raphael to his bower, begs him to taste human
hospitality:

> '... unsavourie food perhaps
> To spiritual Natures; only this I know,
> That one Celestial Father gives to all.'
> To whom the Angel: 'Therefore what he gives
> (Whose praise be ever sung) to man in part
> Spiritual, may of purest Spirits be found
> No ingrateful food.'

All this is very proper. But the Angel then proceeds to volunteer the information that not only is the food not 'unsavourie', but also that celestial organisms like his own can

> . . . smell, touch, taste,
> Tasting concoct, digest, assimilate,
> And corporeal to incorporeal turn.

This, being presented as so intimately personal a matter, is a trifle embarrassing. However, it may pass, since Raphael, with what Beatrice would call his 'infallible advisement' may know that Adam is bursting with curiosity on a subject to which he is too polite to refer. He concludes by answering the question Adam did ask:

> '. . . and to taste
> Think not I shall be nice'. So down they sat,
> And to their viands fell.

And there it would have been well to leave it. But Milton, having a bone to pick with the theologians, cannot leave the thing alone, and repeats that Raphael's eating was not done 'seemingly or in mist'

> but with keen dispatch
> Of real hunger, and concoctive heate
> To transubstantiate: what redounds, transpires
> Through Spirits with ease . . .

But here the reader's good manners rise up in protest. We resent being compelled to inspect a gentleman's interior plumbing while he is at lunch. Earlier, later, or elsewhere, we should be deeply interested, but not at table.

Milton has often been derided for the unconscious humour of this passage, which is variously attributed to his pompous euphemism, or his over-materialistic angelology, or to other sins which he has not committed. As a matter of fact there is nothing whatever wrong with the passage except faulty timing and placing; and from that, indeed, a livelier sense of comedy would have saved him.

Much the same thing happens in another pair of parallel passages. Some laughter, and some rebuke, have been aimed at Milton for his wounded angels whose 'ethereal substance closed, not long divisible'; yet Dante has used the same device and, so far as I know, got away with it unreproved. But Dante has kept this piece of grotesque futility for the Circle of the

Schismatics, where it is highly relevant, and extremely suitable
to the vain repetitions and meaningless monotony of Hell.
Milton has introduced us to it in Heaven, and, what is worse,
thrust it into the middle of a battle, where it holds up the action
—as though Dante had delayed the mad rush over the cliff
of the Sixth Bolgia to explain how Virgil was able to lift him.
And once again Milton might have carried the thing off
triumphantly if he had not harped upon it; nothing could
be more splendid than:

> then Satan first knew pain,
> And writh'd him to and fro convolv'd; so sore
> The griding sword with discontinuous wound
> Pass'd through him . . .

But he cannot leave it alone, and starts again a dozen lines
further down:

> for Spirits that live throughout
> Vital in every part . . .

It is too much; we must have *either* a battle *or* an explanation—
we cannot with propriety have both at once. If only the
explanation could have been worked in at some earlier point,
then the mention of the griding sword and discontinuous wound
would have sufficed superbly for the combat. Dante's fable
called for no celestial wars, therefore he was able to place the
non-divisibility of ethereal substance in Hell and leave it there.
In his adult and intellectual Heaven such things have no place;
he is even careful explicitly to exclude from it all weights and
measures, including his own:

> S'io era sol di me quel che creasti
> novellamente, Amor che il ciel governi,
> tu il sai, che col tuo lume mi levasti.[1]

(If I then became only that part of me which thou didst new
create, O Love that rulest Heaven, thou knowest, that didst uplift
me with thy light.)

---

[1] Similarly, by removing even the appearance of human form from all the
blissful souls between the Second Heaven and the Empyrean, Dante's tact avoids
the unfortunate implications suggested by Raphael's

> smile that glowed
> Celestial rosie red, Love's proper hue,

on being asked whether heavenly spirits expressed their love

> . . . by looks onely, or do they mix
> Irradiance, virtual or immediate touch?

[*Note continued on page* 28

And having thus got Dante, with or without his body, into Heaven, I find myself faced with analysing a piece of narrative craftsmanship which almost defies analysis. It is the manner in which the very technique of the telling mirrors in itself the actual content of the poem.

Of the examples which came readily to my hand to illustrate the processes of Dante's craftsmanship the *Inferno* offered the greatest number, the *Purgatorio* the next greatest, and the *Paradiso* the fewest. That is not because the poet's skill grew less as he went on. Far from it. But in the *Inferno* the 'tricks of the trade' (if one may call them so in no disparaging sense) find their most obvious and concrete expressions. The poet has presented himself with a richly romantic landscape full of picturesque inventions, and has used this material to the full. There is, rightly, a grossness in Hell, and, corresponding to it, there is a certain crowded and close-grained quality in the workmanship. But as the soul ascends Mount Purgatory, it strips off grossness; the poetry effects this purging in two ways simultaneously. Directly, of course, it effects it by an immediate change of atmosphere and colour. If the interior of Hell is like a painting by Michael Angelo, the wind- and sea-swept exterior of Mount Purgatory is like a painting by Perugino. The loveliness of the sky, passing from the 'dolce color d'oriental zaffiro' to the shifting hues of dawn, the dew-drenched grass and sway-

Note continued from page 27]

I doubt whether Milton intended this to be a 'blush' in our rather simpering sense of the word. He probably meant to express something more like

> L'altra letizia, che m'era già nota
> preclara cosa, mi si fece in vista
> qual fin balascio in che lo sol percota.
> Per letiziar lassù folgor s'acquista,
> Si come riso qui . . .

(The other [spirit of] joy, already apparent to me as a thing outshining, became to my eyes like a fine ruby smitten by the sun; joy up there declares itself by greater brightness, as here by a smile . . .)

But the human shape, the previous insistence on the material concoction and evacuation, and the stress laid in the present passage on the materiality of angelic forms, compel the imagination, no matter how carefully the hypothesis of total interpenetrability is worded. What we cannot help *seeing* is a human figure going self-consciously red in the face. It is noteworthy that when the human form disappears from the *Paradiso* it does so, quietly and without comment, precisely in the sphere of Venus. Not even to annoy rival theologians or to rub in the glorious sanctity of the flesh was Dante going to take any chances with the commonness of the common reader; the Florentine exile was a man of the world.

ing reeds, the faint shimmering of the sea, the boat, seen through the mist like Mars rising, and gradually revealing the white wings of the heavenly pilot, the eager souls singing as they come and gladly leaping to the shore—the whole picture is of a translucent and tender and unearthly beauty so utterly unlike anything in the *Inferno* that the sense of relief and escape is almost physical. Equally lovely, though touched in with slightly stronger tints, is the Valley of the Rulers, with its enamelled flowers, green-robed angels, and the sliding glitter of the snake. The landscape, as well as the poetry and the 'feel' of the first eight cantos of the *Purgatorio*, is of a quality so rare and strange that criticism has invented no suitable language to describe it. That is the *direct* mirroring of the process of purgation. But from the moment that we ascend the three steps and pass the actual gate of Purgatory, the second, indirect, mirroring begins. It may perhaps be best expressed by saying that the poetic technique itself begins to strip off its adventitious aids.

Dante's narrative power of excitement, his speed, precision, humour and so on, do not depend upon the piling up of Gothic landscapes or the multiplication of agitating incidents. Between the mysterious and lovely shore at the Mountain's foot and the mysterious and lovely wood at its summit there is nothing one can really call landscape—unless one counts the sculptures on the First Cornice, a couple of trees on the Sixth, and one or two beautiful night-sky effects. Nor, except for the earthquake and the meeting with Statius, is there any agitating incident until the plunge through the fire; at most we share Virgil's mild uncertainty whether he is going round the Mountain the right way and his passing anxiety that Dante shall not inadvertently fall over the edge of the cliff. Yet we know the Terraces and Cornices as intimately and accurately as the Infernal Circles. So, too, we know the characters: yet our attention is less, as it were, distracted by them: attention is beginning to sharpen and focus itself towards the crisis of separation and reunion. Virgil— so soon to be withdrawn—is closer to Dante and to us; in Hell he was usually 'il duca', 'il mio dottore', 'il maestro', and was only once or twice called by his name, and that towards the end of the descent; now the verse rings like a chime of bells with: 'Virgilio . . . Virgilio'. And the expectation of Beatrice, no longer remote but imminent, begins to modify the relationship: 'If my words have put you in a perplexity which I cannot resolve

for you, do not be content till you have had it all explained
by her
             che lume fia tra il vero e l'intelletto.
          Non so se intendi: io dico di Beatrice;

(who shall be the light between truth and intellect. I do not know
whether you understand me: I mean Beatrice)

                     Quanto ragion qui vede
          dirti poss' io; da indi in là t'aspetta
          pure a Beatrice, ch'opera è di fede.

(So far as intellect sees here, I can tell you; from that point on you
must look only to Beatrice, for it is matter of faith.)

          Lo dolce padre mio, per confortarmi,
             pur di Beatrice ragionando andava.

(To encourage me, my sweet father talked as he went only of
Beatrice.)

The comedy has lost its harsher and deeper notes, but is no
less comedy for that; just as the *Egoist* or *Pride and Prejudice* is
no less filled with the comic spirit than *Tom Jones* or *Don Juan*,
though remaining consistently on one high, sweet, subtle, and
civilized level. Laughter is able, at the poet's will, to maintain
itself out of its own resources, without special apparatus of
grotesques and comic turns. The narrator's art *si raccoglie*.
Growing as a tree grows, organically, into self-contained shape-
liness, it dispenses with exterior props, and the poem, like the
pilgrim, is crowned and mitred over itself.

In the *Paradiso* the liberation is completed. In so far as it is
possible for a narrative style to be 'transhumanized', the thing is
done. Landscape vanishes: there is nothing that could be called
so, except the vertiginous visual plunge from Gemini over the
Seven Spheres to the tiny threshing-floor which is the Earth.
The River of Life—the last of Dante's great rivers—is not
'landscape' except as it recalls those other rivers of Hell and the
Earthly Paradise; it is visioned Time, as the Rose into which
it transmutes itself is visioned Eternity. The whole outward
aspect of things is resolved into light and motion; 'landscape'
becomes a dance of geometrical patterns, touched in from a
palette of pure light. From the nacreous sheen of Luna, past the
triple coronal of the Sun, and the Cross of Mars, and the Eagle
of Jupiter, up to that infinitesimal point from which

          depende il cielo e tutta la natura,

          (Heaven and all nature hangs,)

we have traversed these lucidities, and know them as intimately
as we knew the granite cliffs of Malebolge; precision and particularity are still there; the romantic method remains, but
instead of working through the customary pictorial parapher-
nalia it is directed to the primary forms.

The human outline vanishes, its place taken by the living
lights which 'nestle in their own brightness'. Of Beatrice herself
we are shown only the eyes and the smile and, once, the wave
of a wafting hand. The other characters are known to us no
longer by look and gesture, but by voice and word—by intellectual being; as God is One with His Word, so they, in their
degree, are what they speak.

Incident vanishes; in the *Paradiso* no *event*, in the ordinary
sense of the word, takes place. There is only the soaring flight
into Heaven after Heaven—all of which (it is explained to us)
are in fact one and the same Heaven; a continuous pressing
closer to the heart of reality. The excitement, once maintained
by encounters with monsters, by perils and escapes, by peripeteia and 'strange surprising adventures', is now transmuted
into a steadily increasing exhilaration, a piling-up of that *stupor*
which, as a younger Dante had pointed out, comes over us in
the presence of great and wonderful things. It was surprising
to crane over the Great Barrier and see Geryon come slowly
swimming up through the thick air: it is surprising also to gaze up
at the Eagle of Jupiter and see the pagan soul of just Rhipeus
flashing in this Christian Paradise; but the surprise is of another
kind. It is a joy and a wonder to emerge from the din and squalor
of the Pit into the stillness and starlight of Purgatory; but it belongs to a different frame of discourse from the joy and wonder of
that astonishing moment when the singing and circling *trionfo* of
the Hierarchies is 'little by little quenched from sight', leaving
Dante with Beatrice alone in an empty Heaven. The story is
still one of adventure, but it has become purely and simply an
adventure of the passionate intellect. 'As lightning bursts from
the cloud, dilating itself till it can no longer be contained,

> la mente mia così, tra quelle dape
> fatta più grande, di sè stessa uscio,
> e, che si fesse, rimembrar non sape ...

(so my mind, filled to overflowing with this feast, issued forth
from itself, and what it then became knows not how to recall. . . .)
It excites him, and his excitement is infectious.

Excitement about *getting* to Heaven is not rare in works of literature; excitement about *being* in Heaven is a much rarer thing. Few poets venture to linger very long after the first trumpet-blast that heralds the opening of the gates. To devote three-and-thirty cantos to the mere exploration of Paradise, without assistance from celestial conflicts, terrestrial judgements, or Olympian fun and games, is a cracking test of the poet's confidence both in his skill and in his theme. But the thing is done: the possibility of enduring delight is grasped and presented in a way that the adult intellect can accept. And now we can at last understand why Dante's beloved master had to be excluded from this Paradise, and what is meant by the sentence:

> Io son Virgilio; e per null' altro rio
> lo ciel perdei, che per non aver fè.

(I am Virgil; and for no other fault did I lose Heaven, save only that I had not faith.)

Faith is imagination actualized by the will; what was lacking to Virgil's faith was precisely the imagination. To the great heathen Dante has allotted just that beatitude which they were able to imagine for themselves. On the 'enamelled green' within that 'goodly castle' about which

> plurimus Eridani per silvam volvitur amnis

the heroes and sages of Antiquity dwell in a serene, unearthly light, just as Virgil had said:

> largior hic campos aether et lumine vestit
> purpureo, solemque suum, sua sidera norunt.

And here, doubtless, though Dante does not expressly mention it:

> pars in gramineis exercent membra palestris,
> contendunt ludo et fulva luctantur harena;
> pars pedibus plaudunt choreas et carmina dicunt . . .
> stant terra defixae hastae, passimque soluti
> per campam pascuntur equi.

Such was their best imagination; and now from the height of the Empyrean we look down with Dante and recognize it for what it is. Beautiful and peaceful, pathetic and fatigued, 'all passion spent', it is only the upper circle of an immense despair. The *ben dell' intelletto* is here not lost, but it is arrested in an intermin-

able adolescence. The endless games, the shining phantom
horses, the odes and the choric measures are touched with the
eternal futility, the eternal melancholy of Hell. 'With how
many teeth does this love bite you?' asks St. John of Dante. In
the *inania regna* love and all other raptures have had their teeth
drawn. There is no pressure, no driving-power, and, signifi-
cantly, there is no laughter.[1]

Laughter, indeed, does not vanish in the *Paradiso*: it is intensi-
fied. The spheres and the hierarchy whirl, dizzy with delight,
'like a mill-wheel'; angels and rejoicing souls spin and weave
their fantastic dance; it is, one feels, only by a supreme act of
blessed courtesy that they momentarily suspend their celestial
merriment to answer Dante's questions, so eager do they seem
to be off again, hands across and down the middle. Yet to
stand or to go is equally their bliss; they poise, they hover
quivering, they glow, they laugh a little at the simplicity of the
living man, they speak 'joyously', and then

> li santi cerchi mostrar nuova gioia
> nel torneare e nella mira nota.

(the holy circles displayed new joy in their wheeling and in their
wondrous song.)

Beatrice, gently mocking, delicately teasing her *fidele*, draws him
even deeper into the wonder of her smile. 'Look at me.' Indeed
he asks nothing better, and remains entranced. She rounds on
him with enchanting inconsistency:

> Perchè la faccia mia sì t'innamora,
> che tu non ti rivolgi al bel giardino
> che sotto i raggi di Cristo s'infiora?

(Wherefore does my face so enamour you that you will not turn to
that fair garden which blossoms in the rays of Christ?)

She has used hard words to him, she has called him childish-
foolish; but that is only love's way. With a delighted pride, as

---

[1] Dante, as Charles Williams pointed out, could not have let Virgil and the
other great pagans into the Christian heaven without making nonsense of their
work: 'We have more tenderness for them, but Dante had more honour.' One last
service, however, he did perform for his 'master and author'. By a touching and
beautiful act of piety he has taken Virgil's simile of the bees visiting the flowers
and transplanted it from the Elysian Fields to the Empyrean itself (*Aen.* VI. 707–9;
Para. xxxi. 7–12). So long as poetry endures, one image of Virgil is established in
that place where Beatrice, according to her promise, many a time speaks Virgil's
praises to her Saviour.

of a fond mother, or a heavenly schoolmistress with a really exceptional pupil, she presents him to the examiners: 'Tenta costui', she says to St. Peter; and to St. James:

> La Chiesa militante alcun figliuolo
> non ha con più speranza . . .
> Gli altri due punti . . .
> a lui lasc' io; chè non gli saran forti,
> nè di iattanza; ed egli a ciò risponda.

(No son of the Church Militant has more hope than he . . . the other two points I leave to him, for he will not find them hard, nor will he try to show off; so let him answer to this.)

Humanity is not lost, and so even comedy is not lost, as the mirth kindles into a more mysterious ecstasy of glory and all Heaven rejoices

> sì che m'inebbriava il dolce canto.
> Ciò ch'io vedeva, mi sembiava un riso
> dell' universo; per che mia ebbrezza
> entrava per l'udire e per lo viso.

(so that I was made drunken by the sweet song. What I beheld seemed to me like the smile of the whole universe, so that the intoxication entered into me both by sight and hearing.)

This, then, was what he really wanted—sour Dante, grim Dante of the uncompromising profile—this is what he thought reality was like, when you got to the *eterna fontana* at the centre of it: this laughter, this inebriation, this riot of charity and hilarity. Possibly, in the flesh, he did not smile very much upon the universe; certainly, during his twenty years of exile, it had not smiled much on him. But he claimed, rightly, that he had never lost faith in it, nor hope nor love either. He had never thought to blame God for his misfortunes, nor 'blasphemously to inveigh against the creation', and wherever he is now, he is not sprawled upon the burning sand with Capaneus. Out of some inexhaustible spring in his fierce heart this great fountain of happiness comes bursting and bubbling. The *stupor* that we share with Dante, thus 'from glory unto glory advancing', is accompanied by a minor, yet not unworthy, *stupor* at 'the achieve, the mastery of the thing'. It is a marvel to watch mere poetry, mere words, thus go up and up, and to feel such inner certainty that we can trust the poet to take them all the way, the song growing shriller and sweeter the higher it soars:

> quale allodetta che in aere si spazia
> prima cantando, e poi tace contenta
> dell' ultima dolcezza che la sazia.

(like the lark, which soars into the sky, singing at first, and then is silent, content with that ultimate sweetness which fills her to the full.)

With Dante it is for once not true that to travel hopefully is better than to arrive. We arrive, and the arrival is satisfactory. The adventure of the passionate intellect is achieved, and it is so because Dante's passions really are seated in his intellect, and not, as with so many of us, marooned in his heart and liver, without means of access to the brain. On whatever rarefied flights the story-teller sets out, he can take his whole equipment with him.

This accounts for a phenomenon which shocks some readers as much as it transports others. Throughout the entire *Comedy* one thing remains constant: the quality of the similes. They are all brief and all directly functional,[1] and from first to last they are earthy, homely, and concrete. Driven at close intervals into the fabric of the poem, they stud the surface like strong holding-pins, pegging it immovably to daily experience, and super-imposing on its flowing pattern an all-over diaper of their own. Considered in themselves they are astonishingly varied, ranging from the coarsest to the most delicate, and from the ridiculous to the sublime; but this variety does not coincide with the pro-gressive variation of the poetic treatment. We do not find all the gross similes in the gross bits and all the noble similes in the noble bits; and the images are neither dehumanized in Hell nor transhumanized in Heaven. Almost anything may be likened to almost anything, provided that it is like, and that we shall follow the story better for seeing the likeness. The lovely similes of the fireflies, and the chariot of Elijah—'la fiamma sola, si come nuvoletta'—occur in the Eighth Bolgia; in the Eighth Heaven the form of our great First Father, hidden in the light

---

[1] That is, they all directly illuminate the story by supplying a real likeness for the object or action described. They are never 'fudged in' for the *sole* purpose of creating a mood or an atmosphere, although they frequently do this as well. Compare, for example, the handling of the phoenix-simile which trails a whiff of incense across the squalors of the Seventh Bolgia (*Inf.* xxiv. 106–11) with that of the fish-stink parallel which performs an equal and opposite office in *Paradise Lost*, iv. 166–71.

that veils it (as those other spirits are shrouded in the fire of
their own torment) makes itself guessed—how? like something
one might see in any market town:

> Tal volta un animal coperto broglia
> sì che l'affetto convien che si paia
> per lo seguir che face a lui l'invoglia.

(Sometimes a covered-up animal wriggles, so that its movements
are outlined by the upheavals of the sacking which follow them.)

It was like that, says Dante, anxious that we should get this
rather difficult picture clear, and caring nothing for the out-
raged susceptibilities of Mr. John Addington Symonds. In the
Heaven of Mars, the noble Maccabaeus flashes and spins, 'e
letizia era ferza del paleo—and joy was the whip to the top'. On
Mount Purgatory the souls importune Dante for his prayers,
like the hangers-on who cluster round a successful gambler.
In Hell the lost lovers wheel like starlings and drop like doves;
and deep in the filthy circle of disease and madness two leprous
horrors sit propped together domestically, 'like a couple of pans
set to warm by the fire'. Fish, frogs, insects, beasts, and birds of
every description flit and gambol through all the circles of the
Three Kingdoms; cooks, tailors, blacksmiths, shepherds, and
seamen ply their trades indiscriminately in deep Hell or high
Heaven, and flowers spring up in the most unexpected places.
But this unity-in-diversity of the incidental imagery is only
made appropriate or possible by the massive unity of the poem
itself; and this is something which we cannot perceive unless
we read the thing properly, from start to finish, as a story should
be read. An anthology of the 'beauties of Dante' would exclude
the architectural beauty which is the poem's chief glory, and
would successfully prevent the full appreciation even of such
beauties as it did include. Even artistically, the powerful sub-
structure of the *Inferno* appears objectless until we see the great
leaping shafts and pinnacles it was built to carry; consequently,
those who spend their whole time grubbing about the vaults of the
Comedy rather naturally carry away with them little impression
of Dante except a grimness of heavy stone and a savour of decay.
But it would be equally disastrous if a fashion for 'spirituality'
and a reluctance to believe in judgement should swing us to the
opposite extreme, and cause the *Inferno* to be boycotted in its
turn; for, even artistically, it is impossible to appreciate the

narrative method of the *Paradiso* unless we see just what it is that has been thus transhumanized and transmuted into air and fire. 'Begin at the beginning', said the King of Hearts, very properly, 'and go on till you come to the end; then stop.' Having done this once, we can, of course, go back and linger over the bits we like best, or begin all over again; but a story is a story and our first acquaintance with it should not be made higgledy-piggledy or back to front. That is not the author's intention; if it had been he would have written something else— a bunch of lyrics, or a Manual of Devotions, or a Handy Guide to Trecento Politics, or a series of Pen-portraits of Medieval Celebrities. The *Comedy* is none of these things: it is a story. It is called a 'comedy', says Dante, because 'if we have respect to its content, at the beginning it is horrible and fetid, for it is Hell; and in the end it is prosperous, desirable and gracious, for it is Paradise'. And, having by singular good fortune contrived to make its acquaintance in the order, and under the aspect, intended by its creator, I find myself disposed to echo the verdict of the three obnoxious children in the Saki story mentioned above:

'The story began badly,' said the smaller of the small girls, 'but it had a beautiful ending.'

'It is the most beautiful that I ever heard,' said the bigger of the small girls, with immense decision.

'It is the *only* beautiful story I have ever heard,' said Cyril.

NOTE.—Quotations throughout are taken from the text printed in the Temple Classics edition.

ON FAIRY-STORIES

J. R. R. TOLKIEN

THIS essay was originally intended to be one of the Andrew Lang lectures at St. Andrews, and it was, in abbreviated form, delivered there in 1938. To be invited to lecture in St. Andrews is a high compliment to any man; to be allowed to speak about fairy-stories is (for an Englishman in Scotland) a perilous honour. I felt like a conjuror who finds himself, by some mistake, called upon to give a display of magic before the court of an elf-king. After producing his rabbit, such a clumsy performer may consider himself lucky, if he is allowed to go home in his proper shape, or indeed to go home at all. There are dungeons in fairyland for the overbold.

And overbold I fear I may be accounted, because I am a reader and lover of fairy-stories, but not a student of them, as Andrew Lang was. I have not the learning, nor the still more necessary wisdom, which the subject demands. The land of fairy-story is wide and deep and high, and is filled with many things: all manner of beasts and birds are found there; shoreless seas and stars uncounted; beauty that is an enchantment, and an ever-present peril; both sorrow and joy as sharp as swords. In that land a man may (perhaps) count himself fortunate to have wandered, but its very richness and strangeness make dumb the traveller who would report it. And while he is there it is dangerous for him to ask too many questions, lest the gates shut and the keys be lost. The fairy gold too often turns to withered leaves when it is brought away. All that I can ask is that you, knowing these things, will receive my withered leaves, as a token that my hand at least once held a little of the gold.

But there are some questions that one who is to speak about fairy-stories cannot help asking, whatever the folk of Faërie think of him or do to him. For instance: What are fairy-stories? What is their origin? What is the use of them? I will try to give answers to these questions, or rather the broken hints of answers to them that I have gleaned—primarily from the stories themselves: such few of their multitude as I know.

What is a fairy-story? It is in this case no good hastening to the *Oxford English Dictionary*, because it will not tell you. It contains no reference to the combination *fairy-story*, and is unhelpful on the subject of *fairies* generally: volume F was not edited by a Scotsman. In the Supplement, *fairy-tale* is recorded since the year 1750, and its leading sense is said to be (*a*) a tale about fairies, or generally a fairy legend; with developed senses, (*b*) an unreal or incredible story, and (*c*) a falsehood.

The last two senses would obviously make my topic hopelessly vast. But the first sense is too narrow. Not too narrow for a lecture (it is large enough for fifty), but too narrow to cover actual usage. Especially so, if we accept the lexicographer's definition of *fairies*: 'supernatural beings of diminutive size, in popular belief supposed to possess magical powers and to have great influence for good or evil over the affairs of man'.

Supernatural is a dangerous and difficult word in any of its senses, looser or stricter. But to fairies it can hardly be applied, unless *super* is taken merely as a superlative prefix. For it is man who is, in contrast to fairies, supernatural (and often of diminutive stature); whereas they are natural, far more natural than he. Such is their doom. The road to fairyland is not the road to Heaven; nor even to Hell, I believe, though some have held that it may lead thither indirectly by the Devil's tithe.

> O see ye not yon narrow road
> So thick beset wi' thorns and briers?
> That is the path of Righteousness,
> Though after it but few inquires.
>
> And see ye not yon braid, braid road
> That lies across the lily leven?
> That is the path of Wickedness,
> Though some call it the Road to Heaven.
>
> And see ye not yon bonny road
> That winds about yon fernie brae?
> That is the road to fair Elfland,
> Where thou and I this night maun gae.

As for *diminutive size*: I do not deny that that notion is a leading one in modern use. I have often thought that it would be interesting to try to find out how that has come to be so; but my knowledge is not sufficient for a certain answer. Of old there were indeed some inhabitants of Faërie that were small (though hardly diminutive), but smallness was not characteristic of that people as a whole. The diminutive being, elf or fairy, is (I guess) in England largely a sophisticated product of literary fancy.[1] It is perhaps not unnatural that in England, the land where the love of the delicate and fine has often re-appeared in art, fancy should in this matter turn towards the dainty and diminutive, as in France it went to court and put on powder and diamonds. Yet I suspect that this flower-and-butterfly minuteness was also a product of 'rationalization', which transformed the glamour of Elfland into mere finesse, and invisibility into a fragility that could hide in a cowslip or shrink behind a blade of grass. It seems to become fashionable soon after the great voyages had begun to make the world seem too narrow to hold both men and elves; when the magic land of Hy Breasail in the West had become the mere Brazils, the land of red-dye-wood.[2] In any case it was largely a literary business in which William Shakespeare and Michael Drayton played a part.[3] Drayton's *Nymphidia* is one ancestor of that long line of flower-fairies and fluttering sprites with antennae that I so disliked as a child, and which my children in their turn detested. Andrew Lang had similar feelings. In the preface to the *Lilac Fairy Book* he refers to the tales of tiresome contemporary authors: 'they always begin with a little boy or girl who goes out and meets the fairies of polyanthuses and gardenias and apple-blossom. . . . These fairies try to be funny and fail; or they try to preach and succeed.'

But the business began, as I have said, long before the nineteenth century, and long ago achieved tiresomeness, certainly the tiresomeness of trying to be funny and failing. Drayton's *Nymphidia* is, considered as a fairy-story (a story about fairies), one of the worst ever written. The palace of Oberon has walls of spider's legs,

> And windows of the eyes of cats,
> And for the roof, instead of slats,
> Is covered with the wings of bats.

[1] I am speaking of developments before the growth of interest in the folk-lore of other countries. The English words, such as *elf*, have long been influenced by French (from which *fay* and *faërie*, *fairy* are derived); but in later times, through their use in translation, both *fairy* and *elf* have acquired much of the atmosphere of German, Scandinavian, and Celtic tales, and many characteristics of the *huldu-fólk*, the *daoine-sìthe*, and the *tylwyth teg*.

[2] For the probability that the Irish *Hy Breasail* played a part in the naming of Brazil see Nansen, *In Northern Mists*, ii. 223–30.

[3] Their influence was not confined to England. German *Elf, Elfe* appears to be derived from *A Midsummer-night's Dream*, in Wieland's translation (1764).

The knight Pigwiggen rides on a frisky earwig, and sends his love, Queen Mab, a bracelet of emmets' eyes, making an assignation in a cowslip-flower. But the tale that is told amid all this prettiness is a dull story of intrigue and sly go-betweens; the gallant knight and angry husband fall into the mire, and their wrath is stilled by a draught of the waters of Lethe. It would have been better if Lethe had swallowed the whole affair. Oberon, Mab, and Pigwiggen may be diminutive elves or fairies, as Arthur, Guinevere, and Lancelot are not; but the good and evil story of Arthur's court is a 'fairy-story' rather than this tale of Oberon.

Fairy, as a noun more or less equivalent to *elf*, is a relatively modern word, hardly used until the Tudor period. The first quotation in the *Oxford Dictionary* (the only one before A.D. 1400) is significant. It is taken from the poet Gower: *as he were a faierie*. But this Gower did not say. He wrote *as he were of faierie*, 'as if he were come from Faërie'. Gower was describing a young gallant who seeks to bewitch the hearts of the maidens in church.

> His croket kembd and thereon set
> A Nouche with a chapelet,
> Or elles one of grene leves
> Which late com out of the greves,
> Al for he sholde seme freissh;
> And thus he loketh on the fleissh,
> Riht as an hauk which hath a sihte
> Upon the foul ther he schal lihte,
> And as he were of faierie
> He scheweth him tofore here yhe.[1]

This is a young man of mortal blood and bone; but he gives a much better picture of the inhabitants of Elfland than the definition of a 'fairy' under which he is, by a double error, placed. For the trouble with the real folk of Faërie is that they do not always look like what they are; and they put on the pride and beauty that we would fain wear ourselves. At least part of the magic that they wield for the good or evil of man is power to play on the desires of his body and his heart. The Queen of Elfland, who carried off Thomas the Rhymer upon her milk-white steed swifter than the wind, came riding by the Eildon Tree as a lady, if one of enchanting beauty. So that

---

[1] *Confessio Amantis*, v. 7065 ff.

⟨w⟩as in the true tradition when he called the knights of ⟨Faë⟩rie by the name of Elfe. It belonged to such knights as ⟨G⟩uyon rather than to Pigwiggen armed with a hornet's ⟨st⟩ing.

Now, though I have only touched (wholly inadequately) on *elves* and *fairies*, I must turn back; for I have digressed from my proper theme: fairy-stories. I said the sense 'stories about fairies' was too narrow.[1] It is too narrow, even if we reject the diminutive size, for fairy-stories are not in normal English usage stories *about* fairies or elves, but stories about Fairy, that is *Faërie*, the realm or state in which fairies have their being. *Faërie* contains many things besides elves and fays, and besides dwarfs, witches, trolls, giants, or dragons: it holds the seas, the sun, the moon, the sky; and the earth, and all things that are in it: tree and bird, water and stone, wine and bread, and ourselves, mortal men, when we are enchanted.

Stories that are actually concerned primarily with 'fairies', that is with creatures that might also in modern English be called 'elves', are relatively rare, and as a rule not very interesting. Most good 'fairy-stories' are about the *aventures* of men in the Perilous Realm or upon its shadowy marches. Naturally so; for if elves are true, and really exist independently of our tales about them, then this also is certainly true: elves are not primarily concerned with us, nor we with them. Our fates are sundered, and our paths seldom meet. Even upon the borders of Faërie we encounter them only at some chance crossing of the ways.[2]

The definition of a fairy-story—what it is, or what it should be—does not, then, depend on any definition or historical account of elf or fairy, but upon the nature of *Faërie*: the Perilous Realm itself, and the air that blows in that country. I will not attempt to define that, nor to describe it directly. It cannot be done. Faërie cannot be caught in a net of words; for it is one of its qualities to be indescribable, though not imperceptible. It has many ingredients, but analysis will not necessarily dis-

[1] Except in special cases such as collections of Welsh or Gaelic tales. In these the stories about the 'Fair Family' or the Shee-folk are sometimes distinguished as 'fairy-tales' from 'folk-tales' concerning other marvels. In this use 'fairy-tales' or 'fairy-lore' are usually short accounts of the appearances of 'fairies' or their intrusions upon the affairs of men. But this distinction is a product of translation.

[2] This is true also, even if they are only creations of Man's mind, 'true' only as reflecting in a particular way one of Man's visions of Truth.

cover the secret of the whole. Yet I hope that what I have later
to say about the other questions will give some glimpses of my
own imperfect vision of it. For the moment I will say only this:
a 'fairy-story' is one which touches on or uses Faërie, whatever
its own main purpose may be: satire, adventure, morality,
fantasy. Faërie itself may perhaps most nearly be translated by
Magic[1]—but it is magic of a peculiar mood and power, at the
furthest pole from the vulgar devices of the laborious, scientific,
magician. There is one proviso: if there is any satire present in
the tale, one thing must not be made fun of, the magic itself.
That must in that story be taken seriously, neither laughed at
nor explained away.

But even if we apply only these vague and ill-defined limits,
it becomes plain that many, even the learned in such matters,
have used the term 'fairy-tale' very carelessly. A glance at those
books of recent times that claim to be collections of 'fairy-
stories' is enough to show that tales about fairies, about the fair
family in any of its houses, or even about dwarfs and goblins,
are only a small part of their content. That, as we have seen,
was to be expected. But these books also contain many tales
that do not use, do not even touch upon, Faërie at all; that have
in fact no business to be included.

I will give one or two examples of the expurgations I would
perform. This will assist the negative side of definition. It will
also be found to lead on to the second question: what are the
origins of fairy-stories?

The number of collections of fairy-stories is now very great.
In English none probably rival either the popularity, or the
inclusiveness, or the general merits of the twelve books of twelve
colours which we owe to Andrew Lang and to his wife. The
first of these appeared more than fifty years ago (1889), and is
still in print. Most of its contents pass the test, more or less
clearly. I will not analyse them, though an analysis might be
interesting, but I note in passing that of the stories in this *Blue
Fairy Book* none are primarily about 'fairies', few refer to them.
Most of the tales are taken from French sources: a just choice in
some ways at that time, as perhaps it would be still (though not
to my taste, now or in childhood). At any rate, so powerful has
been the influence of Charles Perrault, since his *Contes de ma
Mère l'Oye* were first Englished in the eighteenth century, and

[1] See further below, p. 70.

of such other excerpts from the vast storehouse of the *Cabinet des Fées* as have become well known, that still, I suppose, if you asked a man to name at random a typical 'fairy story', he would be most likely to name one of these French things: such as *Puss-in-Boots*, *Cinderella*, or *Little Red Riding Hood*. With some people *Grimm's Fairy Tales* might come first to mind.

But what is to be said of the appearance in the *Blue Fairy Book* of *A Voyage to Lilliput*? I will say this: it is *not* a fairy-story, neither as its author made it, nor as it here appears 'condensed' by Miss May Kendall. It has no business in this place. I fear that it was included merely because Lilliputians are small, even diminutive—the only way in which they are at all remarkable. But smallness is in Faërie, as in our world, only an accident. Pygmies are no nearer to fairies than are Patagonians. I do not rule this story out because of its satirical intent: there is satire, sustained or intermittent, in undoubted fairy-stories, and satire may often have been intended in traditional tales where we do not now perceive it. I rule it out, because the vehicle of the satire, brilliant invention though it be, belongs to the class of travellers' tales. Such tales report many marvels, but they are marvels to be seen in this mortal world in some region of our own time and space; distance alone conceals them. The tales of Gulliver have no more right of entry than the yarns of Baron Munchausen; or than, say, *The First Men in the Moon* or *The Time-Machine*. Indeed, for the Eloi and the Morlocks there would be a better claim than for the Lilliputians. Lilliputians are merely men peered down at, sardonically, from just above the house-tops. Eloi and Morlocks live far away in an abyss of time so deep as to work an enchantment upon them; and if they are descended from ourselves, it may be remembered that an ancient English thinker once derived the *ylfe*, the very elves, through Cain from Adam.[1] This enchantment of distance, especially of distant time, is weakened only by the preposterous and incredible Time Machine itself. But we see in this example one of the main reasons why the borders of fairy-story are inevitably dubious. The magic of Faërie is not an end in itself, its virtue is in its operations: among these are the satisfaction of certain primordial human desires. One of these desires is to survey the depths of space and time. Another is (as will be seen) to hold communion with other living things. A story may thus deal

[1] *Beowulf*, 111–12.

with the satisfaction of these desires, with or without the operation of either machine or magic, and in proportion as it succeeds it will approach the quality and have the flavour of
fairy-story.

Next, after travellers' tales, I would also exclude, or rule out
of order, any story that uses the machinery of Dream, the
dreaming of actual human sleep, to explain the apparent occur-
rence of its marvels. At the least, even if the reported dream
was in other respects in itself a fairy-story, I would condemn
the whole as gravely defective: like a good picture in a dis-
figuring frame. It is true that Dream is not unconnected with
Faërie. In dreams strange powers of the mind may be unlocked.
In some of them a man may for a space wield the power of
Faërie, that power which, even as it conceives the story, causes
it to take living form and colour before the eyes. A real dream
may indeed sometimes be a fairy-story of almost elvish ease and
skill—while it is being dreamed. But if a waking writer tells
you that his tale is only a thing imagined in his sleep, he cheats
deliberately the primal desire at the heart of Faërie: the realization, independent of the conceiving mind, of imagined wonder.
It is often reported of fairies (truly or lyingly, I do not know)
that they are workers of illusion, that they are cheaters of men
by 'fantasy'; but that is quite another matter. That is their
affair. Such trickeries happen, at any rate, inside tales in which
the fairies are not themselves illusions: behind the fantasy real
wills and powers exist, independent of the minds and purposes
of men.

It is at any rate essential to a genuine fairy-story, as distinct
from the employment of this form for lesser or debased purposes,
that it should be presented as 'true'. The meaning of 'true' in
this connexion I will consider in a moment. But since the fairy-
story deals with 'marvels', it cannot tolerate any frame or
machinery suggesting that the whole story in which they occur
is a figment or illusion. The tale itself may, of course, be so good
that one can ignore the frame. Or it may be successful and
amusing as a dream-story. So are Lewis Carroll's *Alice* stories,
with their dream-frame and dream-transitions. For this (and
other reasons) they are not fairy-stories.[1]

There is another type of marvellous tale that I would exclude
from the title 'fairy-story', again certainly not because I do not

[1] See Note A at the end (p. 84).

like it: namely pure 'Beast-fable'. I will choose an example from Lang's Fairy Books: *The Monkey's Heart*, a Swahili tale which is given in the *Lilac Fairy Book*. In this story a wicked shark tricked a monkey into riding on his back, and carried him half-way to his own land, before he revealed the fact that the sultan of that country was sick and needed a monkey's heart to cure his disease. But the monkey outwitted the shark, and induced him to return by convincing him that the heart had been left behind at home, hanging in a bag on a tree.

The beast-fable has, of course, a connexion with fairy-stories. Beasts and birds and other creatures often talk like men in real fairy-stories. In some part (often small) this marvel derives from one of the primal 'desires' that lie near the heart of Faërie: the desire of men to hold communion with other living things. But the speech of beasts in the beast-fable, as developed into a separate branch, has little reference to that desire, and often wholly forgets it. The magical understanding by men of the proper languages of birds and beasts and trees, that is much nearer to the true purposes of Faërie. But in stories in which no human being is concerned; or in which the animals are the heroes and heroines, and men and women, if they appear, are mere adjuncts; and above all those in which the animal form is only a mask upon a human face, a device of the satirist or the preacher, in these we have beast-fable and not fairy-story: whether it be *Reynard the Fox*, or *The Nun's Priest's Tale*, or *Brer Rabbit*, or merely *The Three Little Pigs*. The stories of Beatrix Potter lie near the borders of Faërie, but outside it, I think, for the most part.[1] Their nearness is due largely to their strong moral element: by which I mean their inherent morality, not any allegorical *significatio*. But *Peter Rabbit*, though it contains a prohibition, and though there are prohibitions in fairyland (as, probably, there are throughout the universe on every plane and in every dimension), remains a beast-fable.

Now *The Monkey's Heart* is also plainly only a beast-fable. I suspect that its inclusion in a 'Fairy Book' is due not primarily to its entertaining quality, but precisely to the monkey's heart supposed to have been left behind in a bag. That was significant to Lang, the student of folk-lore, even though this curious idea

---

[1] *The Tailor of Gloucester* perhaps comes nearest. *Mrs. Tiggywinkle* would be as near, but for the hinted dream-explanation. I would also include *The Wind in the Willows* in Beast-fable.

is here used only as a joke; for, in this tale, the monkey's heart was in fact quite normal and in his breast. None the less this detail is plainly only a secondary use of an ancient and very widespread folk-lore notion, which does occur in fairy-stories:[1] the notion that the life or strength of a man or creature may reside in some other place or thing; or in some part of the body (especially the heart) that can be detached and hidden in a bag, or under a stone, or in an egg. At one end of recorded folk-lore history this idea was used by George MacDonald in his fairy story *The Giant's Heart*, which derives this central motive (as well as many other details) from well-known traditional tales. At the other end, indeed in what is probably one of the oldest stories in writing, it occurs in *The Tale of the Two Brothers* in the Egyptian D'Orsigny papyrus. There the younger brother says to the elder:

'I shall enchant my heart, and I shall place it upon the top of the flower of the cedar. Now the cedar will be cut down and my heart will fall to the ground, and thou shalt come to seek for it, even though thou pass seven years in seeking it; but when thou hast found it, put it into a vase of cold water, and in very truth I shall live.'[2]

But that point of interest and such comparisons as these bring us to the brink of the second question: What are the origins of 'fairy-stories'? That must, of course, mean: the origin or origins of the fairy elements. To ask what is the origin of stories (however qualified) is to ask what is the origin of language and of the mind.

Actually the question: What is the origin of the fairy element? lands us ultimately in the same fundamental inquiry; but there are many elements in fairy-stories (such as this detachable heart, or swan-robes, magic rings, arbitrary prohibitions, wicked step-mothers, and even fairies themselves) that can be studied without tackling this main question. Such studies are, however, scientific (at least in intent); they are the pursuit of folklorists or anthropologists: that is of people using the stories not as they were meant to be used, but as a quarry from which to dig evidence, or information, about matters in which they are interested. A perfectly legitimate procedure in itself—but

[1] Such as, for instance: *The Giant that had no Heart* in Dasent's *Popular Tales from the Norse*; or *The Sea-Maiden* in Campbell's *Popular Tales of the West Highlands* (no. iv; cf. also no. i); or more remotely *Die Kristallkugel* in Grimm.
[2] Budge, *Egyptian Reading Book*, p. xxi.

ignorance or forgetfulness of the nature of a story (as a thing told in its entirety) has often led such inquirers into strange judgements. To investigators of this sort recurring similarities (such as this matter of the heart) seem specially important. So much so that students of folk-lore are apt to get off their own proper track, or to express themselves in a misleading 'shorthand': misleading in particular, if it gets out of their monographs into books about literature. They are inclined to say that any two stories that are built round the same folk-lore motive, or are made up of a generally similar combination of such motives, are 'the same stories'. We read that *Beowulf* 'is only a version of *Dat Erdmänneken*'; that '*The Black Bull of Norroway* is *Beauty and the Beast*', or 'is the same story as *Eros and Psyche*'; that the Norse *Mastermaid* (or the Gaelic *Battle of the Birds*[1] and its many congeners and variants) is 'the same story as the Greek tale of Jason and Medea'.

Statements of that kind may express (in undue abbreviation) some element of truth; but they are not true in a fairy-story sense, they are not true in art or literature. It is precisely the colouring, the atmosphere, the unclassifiable individual details of a story, and above all the general purport that informs with life the undissected bones of the plot, that really count. Shakespeare's *King Lear* is not the same as Layamon's story in his *Brut*. Or to take the extreme case of *Red Riding Hood*: it is of merely secondary interest that the re-told versions of this story, in which the little girl is saved by wood-cutters, is directly derived from Perrault's story in which she was eaten by the wolf. The really important thing is that the later version has a happy ending (more or less, and if we do not mourn the grandmother overmuch), and that Perrault's version had not. And that is a very profound difference, to which I shall return.

Of course, I do not deny, for I feel strongly, the fascination of the desire to unravel the intricately knotted and ramified history of the branches on the Tree of Tales. It is closely connected with the philologists' study of the tangled skein of Language, of which I know some small pieces. But even with regard to language it seems to me that the essential quality and aptitudes of a given language in a living moment is both more important to seize and far more difficult to make explicit than its linear history. So with regard to fairy stories, I feel that it

[1] See Campbell, op. cit., vol. i.

is more interesting, and also in its way more difficult, to consider what they are, what they have become for us, and what values the long alchemic processes of time have produced in them. In Dasent's words I would say: 'We must be satisfied with the soup that is set before us, and not desire to see the bones of the ox out of which it has been boiled.'[1] Though, oddly enough, Dasent by 'the soup' meant a mishmash of bogus pre-history founded on the early surmises of Comparative Philology; and by 'desire to see the bones' he meant a demand to see the workings and the proofs that led to these theories. By 'the soup' I mean the story as it is served up by its author or teller, and by 'the bones' its sources or material—even when (by rare luck) those can be with certainty discovered. But I do not, of course, forbid criticism of the soup as soup.

I shall therefore pass lightly over the question of origins. I am too unlearned to deal with it in any other way; but it is the least important of the three questions for my purpose, and a few remarks will suffice. It is plain enough that fairy-stories (in wider or in narrower sense) are very ancient indeed. Related things appear in very early records; and they are found universally, wherever there is language. We are therefore obviously confronted with a variant of the problem that the archaeologist encounters, or the comparative philologist: with the debate between *independent evolution* (or rather *invention*) of the similar; *inheritance* from a common ancestry; and *diffusion* at various times from one or more centres. Most debates depend on an attempt (by one or both sides) at over-simplification; and I do not suppose that this debate is an exception. The history of fairy-stories is probably more complex than the physical history of the human race, and as complex as the history of human language. All three things: independent invention, inheritance, and diffusion, have evidently played their part in producing the intricate web of Story. It is now beyond all skill but that of the elves to unravel it.[2] Of these three *invention* is

---

[1] *Popular Tales from the Norse*, p. xviii.

[2] Except in particularly fortunate cases; or in a few occasional details. It is indeed easier to unravel a single *thread*—an incident, a name, a motive—than to trace the history of any *picture* defined by many threads. For with the picture in the tapestry a new element has come in: the picture is greater than, and not explained by, the sum of the component threads. Therein lies the inherent weakness of the analytic (or 'scientific') method: it finds out much about things that occur in stories, but little or nothing about their effect in any given story.

the most important and fundamental, and so (not surprisingly) also the most mysterious. To an inventor, that is to a story-maker, the other two must in the end lead back. *Diffusion* (borrowing in space) whether of an artefact or a story, only refers the problem of origin elsewhere. At the centre of the supposed diffusion there is a place where once an inventor lived. Similarly with *inheritance* (borrowing in time): in this way we arrive at last only at an ancestral inventor. While if we believe that sometimes there occurred the independent striking out of similar ideas and themes or devices, we simply multiply the ancestral inventor but do not in that way the more clearly understand his gift.

Philology has been dethroned from the high place it once had in this court of inquiry. Max Müller's view of mythology as a 'disease of language' can be abandoned without regret. Mythology is not a disease at all, though it may like all human things become diseased. You might as well say that thinking is a disease of the mind. It would be more near the truth to say that languages, especially modern European languages, are a disease of mythology. But Language cannot, all the same, be dismissed. The incarnate mind, the tongue, and the tale are in our world coeval. The human mind, endowed with the powers of generalization and abstraction, sees not only *green-grass*, discriminating it from other things (and finding it fair to look upon), but sees that it is *green* as well as being *grass*. But how powerful, how stimulating to the very faculty that produced it, was the invention of the adjective: no spell or incantation in Faërie is more potent. And that is not surprising: such incantations might indeed be said to be only another view of adjectives, a part of speech in a mythical grammar. The mind that thought of *light, heavy, grey, yellow, still, swift*, also conceived of magic that would make heavy things light and able to fly, turn grey lead into yellow gold, and the still rock into swift water. If it could do the one, it could do the other; it inevitably did both. When we can take green from grass, blue from heaven, and red from blood, we have already an enchanter's power—upon one plane; and the desire to wield that power in the world external to our minds awakes. It does not follow that we shall use that power well upon any plane. We may put a deadly green upon a man's face and produce a horror; we may make the rare and terrible blue moon to shine; or we may cause woods to spring with silver leaves and rams to wear fleeces of gold, and put hot fire into the belly of the cold worm. But in such 'fantasy', as it is called, new form is made; Faërie begins; Man becomes a sub-creator.

An essential power of Faërie is thus the power of making immediately effective by the will the visions of 'fantasy'. Not all are beautiful or even wholesome, not at any rate the fantasies of fallen Man. And he has stained the elves who have this power (in verity or fable) with his own stain. This aspect of 'mythology'—sub-creation, rather than either representation or symbolic interpretation of the beauties and terrors of the world—is, I think, too little considered. Is that because it is seen rather in Faërie than upon Olympus? Because it is thought to belong to the 'lower mythology' rather than to the 'higher'? There has been much debate concerning the relations of these things, of *folk-tale* and *myth*; but, even if there had been no debate, the question would require some notice in any consideration of origins, however brief.

At one time it was a dominant view that all such matter was derived from 'nature-myths'. The Olympians were *personifications* of the sun, of dawn, of night, and so on, and all the stories told about them were originally *myths* (*allegories* would have been a better word) of the greater elemental changes and processes of nature. Epic, heroic legend, saga, then localized these stories in real places and humanized them by attributing them to ancestral heroes, mightier than men and yet already men. And finally these legends, dwindling down, became folk-tales, *Märchen*, fairy-stories—nursery-tales.

That would seem to be the truth almost upside down. The nearer the so-called 'nature-myth', or allegory of the large processes of nature, is to its supposed archetype, the less interesting it is, and indeed the less is it of a myth capable of throwing any illumination whatever on the world. Let us assume for the moment, as this theory assumes, that nothing actually exists corresponding to the 'gods' of mythology: no personalities, only astronomical or meteorological objects. Then these natural objects can only be arrayed with a personal significance and glory by a gift, the gift of a person, of a man. Personality can only be derived from a person. The gods may derive their colour and beauty from the high splendours of nature, but it was Man who obtained these for them, abstracted them from sun and moon and cloud; their personality they get direct from him; the shadow or flicker of divinity that is upon them they receive through him from the invisible world, the Supernatural. There is no fundamental distinction between the higher and lower mythologies. Their peoples live, if they live at all, by the same life, just as in the mortal world do kings and peasants.

Let us take what looks like a clear case of Olympian nature-myth: the Norse god Thórr. His name is Thunder, of which Thórr is the Norse form; and it is not difficult to interpret his hammer, Miöllnir, as lightning. Yet Thórr has (as far as our late records go) a very marked character, or personality, which cannot be found in thunder or in lightning, even though some details can, as it were, be related to these natural phenomena: for instance, his red beard, his loud voice and violent temper, his blundering and smashing strength. None the less it is asking a question without much meaning, if we inquire: Which came first, nature-allegories about personalized thunder in the mountains, splitting rocks and trees; or stories about an irascible, not very clever, red-beard farmer, of a strength beyond common measure, a person (in all but mere stature) very like the Northern farmers, the *bœndr* by whom Thórr was chiefly beloved? To a picture of such a man Thórr may be held to have 'dwindled', or from it the god may be held to have been enlarged. But I doubt whether either view is right—not by itself, not if you insist that one of these things must precede the other. It is more reasonable to suppose that the farmer popped up in the very moment when Thunder got a voice and face; that there was a distant growl of thunder in the hills every time a story-teller heard a farmer in a rage.

Thórr must, of course, be reckoned a member of the higher aristocracy of mythology: one of the rulers of the world. Yet the tale that is told of him in *Thrymskvitha* (in the Elder Edda) is certainly just a fairy-story. It is old, as far as Norse poems go, but that is not far back (say A.D. 900 or a little earlier, in this case). But there is no real reason for supposing that this tale is 'unprimitive', at any rate in quality: that is, because it is of folk-tale kind and not very dignified. If we could go backwards in time, the fairy-story might be found to change in details, or to give way to other tales. But there would always be a 'fairy-tale' as long as there was any Thórr. When the fairy-tale ceased, there would be just thunder, which no human ear had yet heard.

Something really 'higher' is occasionally glimpsed in mythology: Divinity, the right to power (as distinct from its possession), the due of worship; in fact 'religion'. Andrew Lang said, and is by some still commended for saying,[1] that mythology and religion (in the strict sense of that word) are two distinct things that have become inextricably entangled, though mythology is in itself almost devoid of religious significance.[2]

Yet these things have in fact become entangled—or maybe they were sundered long ago and have since groped slowly, through a labyrinth of error, through confusion, back towards re-fusion. Even fairy-stories as a whole have three faces: the Mystical towards the Supernatural; the Magical towards Nature; and the Mirror of scorn and pity towards Man. The essential face of Faërie is the middle one, the Magical. But the degree in which the others appear (if at all) is variable, and may be decided by the individual story-teller. The Magical, the fairy-story, may be used as a *Mirour de l'Omme*; and it may (but not so easily) be made a vehicle of Mystery. This at least is what George MacDonald attempted, achieving stories of power and beauty when he succeeded, as in *The Golden Key* (which he called a fairy-tale); and even when he partly failed, as in *Lilith* (which he called a romance).

For a moment let us return to the 'Soup' that I mentioned above. Speaking of the history of stories and especially of fairy-stories we may say that the Pot of Soup, the Cauldron of Story, has always been boiling, and to it have continually been added new bits, dainty and undainty. For this reason, to take a casual example, the fact that a story resembling the one known as *The Goosegirl* (*Die Gänsemagd* in Grimm) is told in the thirteenth century of Bertha Broadfoot, mother of Charlemagne, really proves nothing either way: neither that the story was (in the thirteenth century) descending from Olympus or Asgard by way of an already legendary king of old, on its way to become a *Hausmärchen*; nor that it was on its way

---

[1] For example, by Christopher Dawson in *Progress and Religion*.

[2] This is borne out by the more careful and sympathetic study of 'primitive' peoples: that is, peoples still living in an inherited paganism, who are not, as we say, civilized. The hasty survey finds only their wilder tales; a closer examination finds their cosmological myths; only patience and inner knowledge discovers their philosophy and religion: the truly worshipful, of which the 'gods' are not necessarily an embodiment at all, or only in a variable measure (often decided by the individual).

up. The story is found to be widespread, unattached to the mother of Charlemagne or to any historical character. From this fact by itself we certainly cannot deduce that it is not true of Charlemagne's mother, though that is the kind of deduction that is most frequently made from that kind of evidence. The opinion that the story is not true of Bertha Broadfoot must be founded on something else: on features in the story which the critic's philosophy does not allow to be possible in 'real life', so that he would actually disbelieve the tale, even if it were found nowhere else; or on the existence of good historical evidence that Bertha's actual life was quite different, so that he would disbelieve the tale, even if his philosophy allowed that it was perfectly possible in 'real life'. No one, I fancy, would discredit a story that the Archbishop of Canterbury slipped on a banana skin merely because he found that a similar comic mishap had been reported of many people, and especially of elderly gentlemen of dignity. He might disbelieve the story, if he discovered that in it an angel (or even a fairy) had warned the archbishop that he would slip if he wore gaiters on a Friday. He might also disbelieve the story, if it was stated to have occurred in the period between, say, 1940 and 1945. So much for that. It is an obvious point, and it has been made before; but I venture to make it again (although it is a little beside my present purpose), for it is constantly neglected by those who concern themselves with the origins of tales.

But what of the banana skin? Our business with it really only begins when it has been rejected by historians. It is more useful when it has been thrown away. The historian would be likely to say that the banana-skin story 'became attached to the Archbishop', as he does say on fair evidence that 'the Goosegirl *Märchen* became attached to Bertha.' That way of putting it is harmless enough, in what is commonly known as 'history'. But is it really a good description of what is going on and has gone on in the history of story-making? I do not think so. I think it would be nearer the truth to say that the archbishop became attached to the banana skin, or that Bertha was turned into the Goosegirl. Better still: I would say that Charlemagne's mother and the Archbishop were put into the Pot, in fact got into the Soup. They were just new bits added to the stock. A considerable honour, for in that soup were many things older, more potent, more beautiful, comic, or terrible than they were in themselves (considered simply as figures of history).

It seems fairly plain that Arthur, once historical (but perhaps as such not of great importance), was also put into the Pot. There he was boiled for a long time, together with many other older figures and devices, of mythology and Faërie, and even some other stray bones of history (such as Alfred's defence against the Danes), until he emerged as a King of Faërie. The situation is similar in the great Northern 'Arthurian' court of the Shield-Kings of Denmark, the *Scyldingas* of ancient English tradition. King Hrothgar and his family have many manifest marks of true history, far more than Arthur; yet even in the older (English) accounts of them they are associated with many figures and events of fairy-story: they have been in the Pot. But I refer now to the remnants of the oldest recorded English tales of Faërie (or its borders), in spite of the fact that they are little known in England, not to discuss the turning of the bear-boy into the knight Beowulf, or to explain the intrusion of the ogre Grendel into the royal hall of Hrothgar. I wish to point to something else that these traditions contain: a singularly suggestive example of the relation of the 'fairy-tale element' to gods and kings and nameless men, illustrating (I believe) the view that this element does not rise or fall, but is there, in the Cauldron of Story, waiting for the great figures of Myth and History, and for the yet nameless He or She, waiting for the moment when they are cast into the simmering stew, one by one or all together, without consideration of rank or precedence.

The great enemy of King Hrothgar was Froda, King of the Heathobards. Yet of Hrothgar's daughter Freawaru we hear echoes of a strange tale—not a usual one in Northern heroic legend: the son of the enemy of her house, Ingeld son of Froda, fell in love with her and wedded her, disastrously. But that is extremely interesting and significant. In the background of the ancient feud looms the figure of that god whom the Norsemen called Frey (the Lord) or Yngvi-frey, and the Angles called Ing: a god of the ancient Northern mythology (and religion) of Fertility and Corn. The enmity of the royal houses was connected with the sacred site of a cult of that religion. Ingeld and his father bear names belonging to it. Freawaru herself is named 'Protection of the Lord (of Frey)'. Yet one of the chief things told later (in Old Icelandic) about Frey is the story in

which he falls in love from afar with the daughter of the enemies
of the gods, Gerdr, daughter of the giant Gymir, and weds her.
Does this prove that Ingeld and Freawaru, or their love, are
'merely mythical'? I think not. History often resembles 'Myth',
because they are both ultimately of the same stuff. If indeed
Ingeld and Freawaru never lived, or at least never loved, then
it is ultimately from nameless man and woman that they get
their tale, or rather into whose tale they have entered. They
have been put into the Cauldron, where so many potent things
lie simmering agelong on the fire, among them Love-at-first-
sight. So too of the god. If no young man had ever fallen in
love by chance meeting with a maiden, and found old enmities
to stand between him and his love, then the god Frey would
never have seen Gerdr the giant's daughter from the high-seat
of Odin. But if we speak of a Cauldron, we must not wholly
forget the Cooks. There are many things in the Cauldron, but
the Cooks do not dip in the ladle quite blindly. Their selection is
important. The gods are after all gods, and it is a matter of some
moment what stories are told of them. So we must freely admit
that a tale of love is more likely to be told of a prince in history,
indeed is more likely actually to happen in an historical family
whose traditions are those of golden Frey and the Vanir, rather
than those of Odin the Goth, the Necromancer, glutter of the
crows, Lord of the Slain. Small wonder that *spell* means both
a story told, and a formula of power over living men.

But when we have done all that research—collection and
comparison of the tales of many lands—can do; when we have
explained many of the elements commonly found embedded in
fairy-stories (such as stepmothers, enchanted bears and bulls,
cannibal witches, taboos on names, and the like) as relics of
ancient customs once practised in daily life, or of beliefs once
held as beliefs and not as 'fancies'—there remains still a point
too often forgotten: that is the effect produced *now* by these old
things in the stories as they are.

For one thing they are now *old*, and antiquity has an appeal
in itself. The beauty and horror of *The Juniper Tree* (*Von dem
Machandelboom*), with its exquisite and tragic beginning, the
abominable cannibal stew, the gruesome bones, the gay and
vengeful bird-spirit coming out of a mist that rose from the tree,
has remained with me since childhood; and yet always the chief

flavour of that tale lingering in the memory was not beauty or horror, but distance and a great abyss of time, not measurable even by *twe tusend Johr*. Without the stew and the bones—which children are now too often spared in mollified versions of Grimm[1]—that vision would largely have been lost. I do not think I was harmed by the horror *in the fairy-tale setting*, out of whatever dark beliefs and practices of the past it may have come. Such stories have now a mythical or total (unanalysable) effect, an effect quite independent of the findings of Comparative Folk-lore, and one which it cannot spoil or explain; they open a door on Other Time, and if we pass through, though only for a moment, we stand outside our own time, outside Time itself, maybe.

If we pause, not merely to note that such old elements have been preserved, but to think *how* they have been preserved, we must conclude, I think, that it has happened, often if not always, precisely because of this literary effect. It cannot have been we, or even the brothers Grimm, that first felt it. Fairy-stories are by no means rocky matrices out of which the fossils cannot be prised except by an expert geologist. The ancient elements can be knocked out, or forgotten and dropped out, or replaced by other ingredients with the greatest ease: as any comparison of a story with closely related variants will show. The things that are there must often have been retained (or inserted) because the oral narrators, instinctively or consciously, felt their literary 'significance'.[2] Even where a prohibition in a fairy-story is guessed to be derived from some taboo once practised long ago, it has probably been preserved in the later stages of the tale's history because of the great mythical significance of prohibition. A sense of that significance may indeed have lain behind some of the taboos themselves. Thou shalt not—or else thou shalt depart beggared into endless regret. The gentlest 'nursery-tales' know it. Even Peter Rabbit was forbidden a garden, lost his blue coat, and took sick. The Locked Door stands as an eternal Temptation.

And with that I think we come to the children, and with them to the last and most important of the three questions: what, if any, are the values and functions of fairy-stories *now*? It is often now assumed that children are the natural or the specially

---

[1] They should not be spared it—unless they are spared the whole story until their digestions are stronger.   [2] See Note B at end (p. 85).

appropriate audience for fairy-stories. In describing a fairy-story which they think adults might possibly read for their own entertainment, reviewers frequently indulge in such waggeries as: ' this book is for children from the ages of six to sixty'. But I have never yet seen the puff of a new motor-model that began thus: 'this toy will amuse infants from seventeen to seventy'; though that to my mind would be much more appropriate. Is there any *essential* connexion between children and fairy-stories? Is there any call for comment, if an adult reads them for himself? *Reads* them as tales, that is, not *studies* them as curios. Adults are allowed to collect and study anything, even old theatre-programmes or paper bags.

Among those who still have enough wisdom not to think fairy-stories pernicious, the common opinion seems to be that there is a natural connexion between the minds of children and fairy-stories, of the same order as the connexion between children's bodies and milk. I think this is an error; at best an error of false sentiment, and one that is therefore most often made by those who, for whatever private reason (such as child-lessness), tend to think of children as a special kind of creature, almost a different race, rather than as normal, if immature, members of a particular family, and of the human family at large.

Actually, the association of children and fairy-stories is an accident of our domestic history. Fairy-stories have in the modern lettered world been relegated to the 'nursery', as shabby or old-fashioned furniture is relegated to the play-room, primarily because the adults do not want it, and do not mind if it is misused.[1] It is not the choice of the children which decides this. Children as a class—except in a common lack of experience they are not one—neither like fairy-stories more, nor understand them better than adults do; and no more than they like many other things. They are young and growing, and normally have keen appetites, so the fairy-stories as a rule go down well enough. But in fact only some children, and some adults, have

[1] In the case of stories and other nursery lore, there is also another factor. Wealthier families employed women to look after their children, and the stories were provided by these nurses, who were sometimes in touch with rustic and traditional lore forgotten by their 'betters'. It is long since this source dried up, at any rate in England; but it once had some importance. But again there is no proof of the special fitness of children as the recipients of this vanishing 'folk-lore'. The nurses might just as well (or better) have been left to choose the pictures and furniture.

any special taste for them; and when they have it, it is not exclusive, nor even necessarily dominant. It is a taste, too, that would not appear, I think, very early in childhood without artificial stimulus; it is certainly one that does not decrease but increases with age, if it is innate.

It is true that in recent times fairy-stories have usually been written or 'adapted' for children. But so may music be, or verse, or novels, or history, or scientific manuals. It is a dangerous process, even when it is necessary. It is indeed only saved from disaster by the fact that the arts and sciences are not as a whole relegated to the nursery; the nursery and schoolroom are merely given such tastes and glimpses of the adult thing as seem fit for them in adult opinion (often much mistaken). Any one of these things would, if left altogether in the nursery, become gravely impaired. So would a beautiful table, a good picture, or a useful machine (such as a microscope), be defaced or broken, if it were left long unregarded in a schoolroom. Fairy-stories banished in this way, cut off from a full adult art, would in the end be ruined; indeed in so far as they have been so banished, they have been ruined. All children's books are on a strict judgement poor books. Books written entirely for children are poor even as children's books.[1]

The value of fairy-stories is thus not, in my opinion, to be found by considering children in particular. Collections of fairy-stories are, in fact, by nature attics and lumber-rooms, only by temporary and local custom play-rooms. Their contents are disordered, and often battered, a jumble of different dates, purposes, and tastes; but among them may occasionally be found a thing of permanent virtue: an old work of art, not too much damaged, that only stupidity would ever have stuffed away.

Andrew Lang's *Fairy Books* are not, perhaps, lumber-rooms. They are more like stalls in a rummage-sale. Someone with a duster and a fair eye for things that retain some value has been round the attics and box-rooms. His collections are largely a by-product of his adult study of mythology and folk-lore; but they were made into and presented as books for children.[2] Some of the reasons that Lang gave are worth considering.

[1] See Note C at end (p. 86).
[2] By Lang and his helpers. It is not true of the majority of the contents in their original (or oldest surviving) forms.

The introduction to the first of the series speaks of 'children to whom and for whom they are told'. 'They represent', he says, 'the young age of man true to his early loves, and have his unblunted edge of belief, a fresh appetite for marvels.' ' "Is it true?" ' he says, 'is the great question children ask.'

I suspect that *belief* and *appetite for marvels* are here regarded as identical or as closely related. They are radically different, though the appetite for marvels is not at once or at first differentiated by a growing human mind from its general appetite. It seems fairly clear that Lang was using belief in its ordinary sense: belief that a thing exists or can happen in the real (primary) world. If so, then I fear that Lang's words, stripped of sentiment, can only imply that the teller of marvellous tales to children must, or may, or at any rate does trade on their *credulity*, on the lack of experience which makes it less easy for children to distinguish fact from fiction in particular cases, though the distinction in itself is fundamental to the sane human mind, and to fairy-stories.

Children are capable, of course, of *literary belief*, when the story-maker's art is good enough to produce it. That state of mind has been called 'willing suspension of disbelief'. But this does not seem to me a good description of what happens. What really happens is that the story-maker proves a successful 'sub-creator'. He makes a Secondary World which your mind can enter. Inside it, what he relates is 'true': it accords with the laws of that world. You therefore believe it, while you are, as it were, inside. The moment disbelief arises, the spell is broken; the magic, or rather art, has failed. You are then out in the Primary World again, looking at the little abortive Secondary World from outside. If you are obliged, by kindliness or circumstance, to stay, then disbelief must be suspended (or stifled), otherwise listening and looking would become intolerable. But this suspension of disbelief is a substitute for the genuine thing, a subterfuge we use when condescending to games or make-believe, or when trying (more or less willingly) to find what virtue we can in the work of an art that has for us failed.

A real enthusiast for cricket is in the enchanted state: Secondary Belief. I, when I watch a match, am on the lower level. I can achieve (more or less) willing suspension of disbelief, when I am held there and supported by some other motive that will keep away boredom: for instance, a wild, heraldic, preference for dark blue rather than light. This suspension of disbelief may thus be a somewhat tired, shabby, or sentimental state of mind, and so lean to the 'adult'. I fancy it is often the state of adults in the presence of a fairy-story. They are held there and supported by sentiment (memories of childhood, or notions of what childhood ought to be like); they think they ought to like the tale. But if they really liked it, for itself, they would not have to suspend disbelief: they would believe—in this sense.

Now if Lang had meant anything like this there might have been some truth in his words. It may be argued that it is easier to work the spell with children. Perhaps it is, though I am not sure of this. The appearance that it is so is often, I think, an adult illusion produced by children's humility, their lack of critical experience and vocabulary, and their voracity (proper to their rapid growth). They like or try to like what is given to them: if they do not like it, they cannot well express their dislike or give reasons for it (and so may conceal it); and they like a great mass of different things indiscriminately, without troubling to analyse the planes of their belief. In any case I doubt if this potion—the enchantment of the effective fairy-story—is really one of the kind that becomes 'blunted' by use, less potent after repeated draughts.

' "Is it true?" is the great question children ask', Lang said. They do ask that question, I know; and it is not one to be rashly or idly answered.[1] But that question is hardly evidence of 'unblunted belief', or even of the desire for it. Most often it proceeds from the child's desire to know which kind of literature he is faced with. Children's knowledge of the world is often so small that they cannot judge, off-hand and without help, between the fantastic, the strange (that is rare or remote facts), the nonsensical, and the merely 'grown-up' (that is ordinary things of their parents' world, much of which still remains unexplored). But they recognize the different classes, and may like all of them at times. Of course the borders between them are often fluctuating or confused; but that is not only true for children. We all know the differences in kind, but we are not always sure how to place anything that we hear. A child may

---

[1] Far more often they have asked me: 'Was he good? Was he wicked?' That is, they were more concerned to get the Right side and the Wrong side clear. For that is a question equally important in History and in Faërie.

well believe a report that there are ogres in the next county; many grown-up persons find it easy to believe of another country; and as for another planet, very few adults seem able to imagine it as peopled, if at all, by anything but monsters of iniquity.

Now I was one of the children whom Andrew Lang was addressing—I was born at about the same time as the *Green Fairy Book*—the children for whom he seemed to think that fairy-stories were the equivalent of the adult novel, and of whom he said: 'Their taste remains like the taste of their naked ancestors thousands of years ago; and they seem to like fairy-tales better than history, poetry, geography, or arithmetic.'[1] But do we really know much about those 'naked ancestors', except that they certainly were not naked? *Our fairy-stories, however old certain elements in them may be, are certainly not the same as theirs. Yet if it is assumed that we have fairy-stories because they did, then probably we have history, geography, poetry, and arithmetic because they liked these things too, as far as they could get them, and in so far as they had yet separated the many branches of their general interest in everything.

And as for children of the present day, Lang's description does not fit my own memories, or my experience of children. Lang may have been mistaken about the children he knew, but if he was not, then at any rate children differ considerably, even within the narrow borders of Britain, and such generalizations which treat them as a class (disregarding their individual talents, and the influences of the countryside they live in, and their upbringing) are delusory. I had no special childish 'wish to believe'. I wanted to know. Belief depended on the way in which stories were presented to me, by older people, or by the authors, or on the inherent tone and quality of the tale. But at no time can I remember that the enjoyment of a story was dependent on belief that such things could happen, or had happened, in 'real life'. Fairy-stories were plainly not primarily concerned with possibility, but with desirability. If they awakened *desire*, satisfying it while often whetting it unbearably, they succeeded. It is not necessary to be more explicit here, for I hope to say something later about this desire, a complex of many ingredients, some universal, some particular to modern men (including modern children), or even to certain kinds of

[1] Preface to the *Violet Fairy Book*.

men. I had no desire to have either dreams or adventures like *Alice*, and the account of them merely amused me. I had very little desire to look for buried treasure or fight pirates, and *Treasure Island* left me cool. Red Indians were better: there were bows and arrows (I had and have a wholly unsatisfied desire to shoot well with a bow), and strange languages, and glimpses of an archaic mode of life, and, above all, forests in such stories. But the land of Merlin and Arthur was better than these, and best of all the nameless North of Sigurd of the Völsungs, and the prince of all dragons. Such lands were pre-eminently desirable. I never imagined that the dragon was of the same order as the horse. And that was not solely because I saw horses daily, but never even the footprint of a worm.[1] The dragon had the trade-mark *Of Faërie* written plain upon him. In whatever world he had his being it was an Other-world. Fantasy, the making or glimpsing of Other-worlds, was the heart of the desire of Faërie. I desired dragons with a profound desire. Of course, I in my timid body did not wish to have them in the neighbourhood, intruding into my relatively safe world, in which it was, for instance, possible to read stories in peace of mind, free from fear.[2] But the world that contained even the imagination of Fáfnir was richer and more beautiful, at whatever cost of peril. The dweller in the quiet and fertile plains may hear of the tormented hills and the unharvested sea and long for them in his heart. For the heart is hard though the body be soft.

All the same, important as I now perceive the fairy-story element in early reading to have been, speaking for myself as a child, I can only say that a liking for fairy-stories was not a dominant characteristic of early taste. A real taste for them awoke after 'nursery' days, and after the years, few but long-seeming, between learning to read and going to school. In that (I nearly wrote 'happy' or 'golden', it was really a sad and troublous) time I liked many other things as well, or better: such as history, astronomy, botany, grammar, and etymology. I agreed with Lang's generalized 'children' not at all in principle, and only in some points by accident: I was, for instance, insensitive

[1] See Note D at end (p. 86).

[2] This is, naturally, often enough what children mean when they ask: 'Is it true?' They mean: 'I like this, but is it contemporary? Am I safe in my bed?' The answer: 'There is certainly no dragon in England to-day', is all that they want to hear.

to poetry, and skipped it if it came in tales. Poetry I discovered much later in Latin and Greek, and especially through being made to try and translate English verse into classical verse. A real taste for fairy-stories was wakened by philology on the threshold of manhood, and quickened to full life by war.

I have said, perhaps, more than enough on this point. At least it will be plain that in my opinion fairy-stories should not be *specially* associated with children. They are associated with them: naturally, because children are human and fairy-stories are a natural human taste (though not necessarily a universal one); accidentally, because fairy-stories are a large part of the literary lumber that in latter-day Europe has been stuffed away in attics; unnaturally, because of erroneous sentiment about children, a sentiment that seems to increase with the decline in children.

It is true that the age of childhood-sentiment has produced some delightful books (especially charming, however, to adults) of the fairy kind or near to it; but it has also produced a dreadful undergrowth of stories written or adapted to what was or is conceived to be the measure of children's minds and needs. The old stories are mollified or bowdlerized, instead of being reserved; the imitations are often merely silly, Pigwiggenry without even the intrigue; or patronizing; or (deadliest of all) covertly sniggering, with an eye on the other grown-ups present. I will not accuse Andrew Lang of sniggering, but certainly he smiled to himself, and certainly too often he had an eye on the faces of other clever people over the heads of his child-audience—to the very grave detriment of the *Chronicles of Pantouflia*.

Dasent replied with vigour and justice to the prudish critics of his translations from Norse popular tales. Yet he committed the astonishing folly of particularly *forbidding* children to read the last two in his collection. That a man could study fairy-stories and not learn better than that seems almost incredible. But neither criticism, rejoinder, nor prohibition would have been necessary if children had not unnecessarily been regarded as the inevitable readers of the book.

I do not deny that there is a truth in Andrew Lang's words (sentimental though they may sound): 'He who would enter into the Kingdom of Faërie should have the heart of a little child.' For that possession is necessary to all high adventure, into kingdoms both less and far greater than Faërie. But humility and innocence—these things 'the heart of a child' must mean in such a context—do not necessarily imply an uncritical wonder, nor indeed an uncritical tenderness. Chesterton once remarked that the children in whose company he saw Maeterlinck's *Blue Bird* were dissatisfied 'because it did not end with a Day of Judgement, and it was not revealed to the hero and the heroine that the Dog had been faithful and the Cat faithless'. 'For children', he says, 'are innocent and love justice; while most of us are wicked and naturally prefer mercy.'

Andrew Lang was confused on this point. He was at pains to defend the slaying of the Yellow Dwarf by Prince Ricardo in one of his own fairy-stories. 'I hate cruelty', he said, '. . . but that was in fair fight, sword in hand, and the dwarf, peace to his ashes! died in harness.' Yet it is not clear that 'fair fight' is less cruel than 'fair judgement'; or that piercing a dwarf with a sword is more just than the execution of wicked kings and evil stepmothers—which Lang abjures: he sends the criminals (as he boasts) to retirement on ample pensions. That is mercy untempered by justice. It is true that this plea was not addressed to children but to parents and guardians, to whom Lang was recommending his own *Prince Prigio* and *Prince Ricardo* as suitable for their charges.[1] It is parents and guardians who have classified fairy-stories as *Juvenilia*. And this is a small sample of the falsification of values that results.

If we use *child* in a good sense (it has also legitimately a bad one) we must not allow that to push us into the sentimentality of only using *adult* or *grown-up* in a bad sense (it has also legitimately a good one). The process of growing older is not necessarily allied to growing wickeder, though the two do often happen together. Children are meant to grow up, and not to become Peter Pans. Not to lose innocence and wonder, but to proceed on the appointed journey: that journey upon which it is certainly not better to travel hopefully than to arrive, though we must travel hopefully if we are to arrive. But it is one of the lessons of fairy-stories (if we can speak of the lessons of things that do not lecture) that on callow, lumpish, and selfish youth peril, sorrow, and the shadow of death can bestow dignity, and even sometimes wisdom.

Let us not divide the human race into Eloi and Morlocks:

[1] Preface to the *Lilac Fairy Book*.

pretty children—'elves' as the eighteenth century often idioti-
cally called them—with their fairy-tales (carefully pruned), and
dark Morlocks tending their machines. If fairy-story as a kind
is worth reading at all it is worthy to be written for and read
by adults. They will, of course, put more in and get more out
than children can. Then, as a branch of a genuine art, children
may hope to get fairy-stories fit for them to read and yet within
their measure; as they may hope to get suitable introductions to
poetry, history, and the sciences.

Very well, then. If adults are to read fairy-stories as a natural
branch of literature—neither playing at being children, nor
pretending to be choosing for children, nor being boys who
would not grow up—what are the values and functions of this
kind? That is, I think, the last and most important question.
I have already hinted at some of my answers. First of all: if
written with art, the prime value of fairy-stories will simply
be that value which, as literature, they share with other
literary forms. But fairy-stories offer also, in a peculiar degree
or mode, these things: Fantasy, Recovery, Escape, Consolation,
all things of which children have, as a rule, less need than older
people. Most of them are nowadays very commonly considered to be bad for anybody. I will consider them briefly,
and will begin with *Fantasy*.

The human mind is capable of forming mental images of
things not actually present. The faculty of conceiving the
images is (or was) naturally called Imagination. But in recent
times, in technical not normal language, Imagination has often
been held to be something higher than the mere image-making,
ascribed to the operations of Fancy (a reduced and depreciatory
form of the older word Fantasy); an attempt is thus made to
restrict, I should say misapply, Imagination to 'the power of
giving to ideal creations the inner consistency of reality'.

Ridiculous though it may be for one so ill-instructed to have
an opinion in this critical matter, I venture to think the verbal
distinction philologically inappropriate, and the analysis in-
accurate. The mental power of image-making is one thing, or
aspect; and it should appropriately be called Imagination. The
perception of the image, the grasp of its implications, and the
control, which are necessary to a successful expression, may vary
in vividness and strength: but this is a difference of degree in
Imagination, not a difference in kind. The achievement of the

expression, which gives (or seems to give) 'the inner consistency of reality',[1] is indeed another thing, or aspect, needing another name: Art, the operative link between Imagination and the final result, Sub-creation. For my present purpose I require a word which shall embrace both the Sub-creative Art in itself and a quality of strangeness and wonder in the Expression, derived from the Image: a quality essential to fairy-story. I propose, therefore, to arrogate to myself the powers of Humpty-Dumpty, and to use Fantasy for this purpose: in a sense, that is, which combines with its older and higher use as an equivalent of Imagination the derived notions of 'unreality' (that is, of unlikeness to the Primary World), of freedom from the domination of observed 'fact', in short of the fantastic. I am thus not only aware but glad of the etymological and semantic connexions of *fantasy* with *fantastic*: with images of things that are not only 'not actually present', but which are indeed not to be found in our primary world at all, or are generally believed not to be found there. But while admitting that, I do not assent to the depreciative tone. That the images are of things not in the primary world (if that indeed is possible) is a virtue not a vice. Fantasy (in this sense) is, I think, not a lower but a higher form of Art, indeed the most nearly pure form, and so (when achieved) the most potent.

Fantasy, of course, starts out with an advantage: arresting strangeness. But that advantage has been turned against it, and has contributed to its disrepute. Many people dislike being 'arrested'. They dislike any meddling with the Primary World, or such small glimpses of it as are familiar to them. They, therefore, stupidly and even maliciously confound Fantasy with Dreaming, in which there is no Art;[2] and with mental disorders, in which there is not even control: with delusion and hallucination.

But the error or malice, engendered by disquiet and consequent dislike, is not the only cause of this confusion. Fantasy has also an essential drawback: it is difficult to achieve. Fantasy may be, as I think, not less but more sub-creative; but at any rate it is found in practice that 'the inner consistency of reality' is more difficult to produce, the more unlike are the images and

---

[1] That is: which commands or induces Secondary Belief.
[2] This is not true of all dreams. In some Fantasy seems to take a part. But this is exceptional. Fantasy is a rational not an irrational activity.

the rearrangements of primary material to the actual arrangements of the Primary World. It is easier to produce this kind
of 'reality' with more 'sober' material. Fantasy thus, too often,
remains undeveloped; it is and has been used frivolously, or
only half-seriously, or merely for decoration: it remains merely
'fanciful'. Anyone inheriting the fantastic device of human
language can say *the green sun*. Many can then imagine or
picture it. But that is not enough—though it may already be
a more potent thing than many a 'thumbnail sketch' or 'transcript of life' that receives literary praise.

To make a Secondary World inside which the green sun
will be credible, commanding Secondary Belief, will probably
require labour and thought, and will certainly demand a special
skill, a kind of elvish craft. Few attempt such difficult tasks.
But when they are attempted and in any degree accomplished
then we have a rare achievement of Art: indeed narrative art,
story-making in its primary and most potent mode.

In human art Fantasy is a thing best left to words, to true
literature. In painting, for instance, the visible presentation of
the fantastic image is technically too easy; the hand tends to
outrun the mind, even to overthrow it.[1] Silliness or morbidity
are frequent results. It is a misfortune that Drama, an art
fundamentally distinct from Literature, should so commonly be
considered together with it, or as a branch of it. Among these
misfortunes we may reckon the depreciation of Fantasy. For
in part at least this depreciation is due to the natural desire of
critics to cry up the forms of literature or 'imagination' that
they themselves, innately or by training, prefer. And criticism
in a country that has produced so great a Drama, and possesses
the works of William Shakespeare, tends to be far too dramatic.
But Drama is naturally hostile to Fantasy. Fantasy, even of
the simplest kind, hardly ever succeeds in Drama, when that
is presented as it should be, visibly and audibly acted. Fantastic forms are not to be counterfeited. Men dressed up as
talking animals may achieve buffoonery or mimicry, but they
do not achieve Fantasy. This is, I think, well illustrated by the
failure of the bastard form, pantomime. The nearer it is to
'dramatized fairy-story' the worse it is. It is only tolerable when
the plot and its fantasy are reduced to a mere vestigiary framework for farce, and no 'belief' of any kind in any part of the

[1] See Note E at end (p. 87).

performance is required or expected of anybody. This is, of course, partly due to the fact that the producers of drama have to, or try to, work with mechanism to represent Fantasy or Magic. I once saw a so-called 'children's pantomime', the straight story of *Puss-in-Boots*, with even the metamorphosis of the ogre into a mouse. Had this been mechanically successful it would either have terrified the spectators or else have been just a turn of high-class conjuring. As it was, though done with some ingenuity of lighting, disbelief had not so much to be suspended as hung, drawn, and quartered.

In *Macbeth*, when it is read, I find the witches tolerable: they have a narrative function and some hint of dark significance; though they are vulgarized, poor things of their kind. They are almost intolerable in the play. They would be quite intolerable, if I were not fortified by some memory of them as they are in the story as read. I am told that I should feel differently if I had the mind of the period, with its witch-hunts and witch-trials. But that is to say: if I regarded the witches as possible, indeed likely, in the Primary World; in other words, if they ceased to be 'Fantasy'. That argument concedes the point. To be dissolved, or to be degraded, is the likely fate of Fantasy when a dramatist tries to use it, even such a dramatist as Shakespeare. *Macbeth* is indeed a work by a playwright who ought, at least on this occasion, to have written a story, if he had the skill or patience for that art.

A reason, more important, I think, than the inadequacy of stage-effects, is this: Drama has, of its very nature, already attempted a kind of bogus, or shall I say at least substitute, magic: *the visible and audible presentation of imaginary men in a story*. That is in itself an attempt to counterfeit the magician's wand. To introduce, even with mechanical success, into this quasi-magical secondary world a further fantasy or magic is to demand, as it were, an inner or tertiary world. It is a world too much. To make such a thing may not be impossible. I have never seen it done with success. But at least it cannot be claimed as the proper mode of drama, in which walking and talking people have been found to be the natural instruments of Art and illusion.[1]

For this precise reason—that the characters, and even the scenes, are in Drama not imagined but actually beheld—Drama

[1] See Note F at end (p. 87).

is, even though it uses a similar material (words, verse, plot),
an art fundamentally different from narrative art. Thus, if you
prefer Drama to Literature (as many literary critics plainly do),
or form your critical theories primarily from dramatic critics,
or even from Drama, you are apt to misunderstand pure story-
making, and to constrain it to the limitations of stage-plays.
You are, for instance, likely to prefer characters, even the basest
and dullest, to things. Very little about trees as trees can be got
into a play.

Now 'Faërian Drama'—those plays which according to
abundant records the elves have often presented to men—can
produce Fantasy with a realism and immediacy beyond the
compass of any human mechanism. As a result their usual
effect (upon a man) is to go beyond Secondary Belief. If you
are present at a Faërian drama you yourself are, or think that
you are, bodily inside its Secondary World. The experience
may be very similar to Dreaming and has (it would seem) sometimes (by men) been confounded with it. But in Faërian drama
you are in a dream that some other mind is weaving, and the
knowledge of that alarming fact may slip from your grasp. To
experience *directly* a Secondary World: the potion is too strong,
and you give to it Primary Belief, however marvellous the
events. You are deluded—whether that is the intention of the
elves (always or at any time) is another question. They at any,
rate are not themselves deluded. This is for them a form of Art,
and distinct from Wizardry or Magic, properly so called. They
do not live in it, though they can, perhaps, afford to spend
more time at it than human artists can. The Primary World,
Reality, of elves and men is the same, if differently valued and
perceived.

We need a word for this elvish craft, but all the words that
have been applied to it have been blurred and confused with
other things. Magic is ready to hand, and I have used it above
(p. 43), but I should not have done so: Magic should be
reserved for the operations of the Magician. Art is the human
process that produces by the way (it is not its only or ultimate
object) Secondary Belief. Art of the same sort, if more skilled
and effortless, the elves can also use, or so the reports seem to
show; but the more potent and specially elvish craft I will, for
lack of a less debatable word, call Enchantment. Enchantment
produces a Secondary World into which both designer and

spectator can enter, to the satisfaction of their senses while they are inside; but in its purity it is artistic in desire and purpose. Magic produces, or pretends to produce, an alteration in the Primary World. It does not matter by whom it is said to be practised, fay or mortal, it remains distinct from the other two; it is not an art but a technique; its desire is *power* in this world, domination of things and wills.

To the elvish craft, Enchantment, Fantasy aspires, and when it is successful of all forms of human art most nearly approaches. At the heart of many man-made stories of the elves lies, open or concealed, pure or alloyed, the desire for a living, realized sub-creative art, which (however much it may outwardly resemble it) is inwardly wholly different from the greed for self-centred power which is the mark of the mere Magician. Of this desire the elves, in their better (but still perilous) part, are largely made; and it is from them that we may learn what is the central desire and aspiration of human Fantasy—even if the elves are, all the more in so far as they are, only a product of Fantasy itself. That creative desire is only cheated by counterfeits, whether the innocent but clumsy devices of the human dramatist, or the malevolent frauds of the magicians. In this world it is for men unsatisfiable, and so imperishable. Uncorrupted it does not seek delusion, nor bewitchment and domination; it seeks shared enrichment, partners in making and delight, not slaves.

To many, Fantasy, this sub-creative art which plays strange tricks with the world and all that is in it, combining nouns and redistributing adjectives, has seemed suspect, if not illegitimate. To some it has seemed at least a childish folly, a thing only for peoples or for persons in their youth. As for its legitimacy I will say no more than to quote a brief passage from a letter I once wrote to a man who described myth and fairy-story as 'lies'; though to do him justice he was kind enough and confused enough to call fairy-story making 'Breathing a lie through Silver'.

> 'Dear Sir,' I said—'Although now long estranged,
> Man is not wholly lost nor wholly changed.
> Dis-graced he may be, yet is not de-throned,
> and keeps the rags of lordship once he owned:
> Man, Sub-creator, the refracted Light
> through whom is splintered from a single White

to many hues, and endlessly combined
in living shapes that move from mind to mind.
Though all the crannies of the world we filled
with Elves and Goblins, though we dared to build
Gods and their houses out of dark and light,
and sowed the seed of dragons—'twas our right
(used or misused). That right has not decayed:
we make still by the law in which we're made.

Fantasy is a natural human activity. It certainly does not destroy or even insult Reason; and it does not either blunt the appetite for, nor obscure the perception of, scientific verity. On the contrary. The keener and the clearer is the reason, the better fantasy will it make. If men were ever in a state in which they did not want to know or could not perceive truth (facts or evidence), then Fantasy would languish until they were cured. If they ever get into that state (it would not seem at all impossible), Fantasy will perish, and become Morbid Delusion.

For creative Fantasy is founded upon the hard recognition that things are so in the world as it appears under the sun; on a recognition of fact, but not a slavery to it. So upon logic was founded the nonsense that displays itself in the tales and rhymes of Lewis Carroll. If men really could not distinguish between frogs and men, fairy-stories about frog-kings would not have arisen.

Fantasy can, of course, be carried to excess. It can be ill done. It can be put to evil uses. It may even delude the minds out of which it came. But of what human thing in this fallen world is that not true? Men have conceived not only of elves, but they have imagined gods, and worshipped them, even worshipped those most deformed by their authors' own evil. But they have made false gods out of other materials: their nations, their banners, their monies; even their sciences and their social and economic theories have demanded human sacrifice. *Abusus non tollit usum.* Fantasy remains a human right: we make in our measure and in our derivative mode, because we are made: and not only made, but made in the image and likeness of a Maker.

As for the disabilities of age, that possibly is true. But it is in the main an idea produced by the mere *study* of fairy-stories. The analytic study of fairy-stories is as bad a preparation for the enjoying or the writing of them as would be the historical study of the drama of all lands and times for the enjoyment or writing of stage-plays. (Andrew Lang is, I fear, an example of this.) The study may indeed become depressing. It is easy for the student to feel that with all his labour he is collecting only a few leaves, many of them now torn or decayed, from the countless foliage of the Tree of Tales, with which the Forest of Days is carpeted. It seems vain to add to the litter. Who can design a new leaf? The patterns from bud to unfolding, and the colours from spring to autumn were all discovered by men long ago. But that is not true. The seed of the tree can be re-planted in almost any soil, even in one so smoke-ridden (as Lang said) as that of England. Spring is, of course, not really less beautiful because we have seen or heard of other like events: like events, never from world's beginning to world's end the same event. Each leaf, of oak and ash and thorn, is a unique embodiment of the pattern, and for some eye this very year may be *the* embodiment, the first ever seen and recognized, though oaks have put forth leaves for countless generations of men. We do not, or need not, despair of painting because all lines must be either straight or curved. The combinations may not be infinite (for we are not), but they are innumerable.

It remains true, nevertheless, that we must not in our day be too curious, too anxious to be original. For we *are* older: certainly older than our known ancestors. The days are gone, as Chesterton said, when red, blue, and yellow could be in-vented blindingly in a black and white world. Gone also are the days when from blue and yellow green was made, unique as a new colour. We are far advanced into Chesterton's third stage with its special danger: the danger of becoming knowing, esoteric, privileged, or pretentious; the stage in which red and green are mixed. In this way a rich russet may (perhaps) be produced. Some will call it a drab brown (and they may be right); but in deft blendings it may be a subtle thing, combining the richness of red and the coolness of green. But in any case we cannot go much further, in the vain desire to be more 'original'. If we add another colour the result is likely to be much like mud, or a mere dead slime. Or if we turn from colour-allegory to fantastic beasts: Fantasy can produce many mythical monsters: of man and horse, the centaur; of lion and eagle, the griffin. But as Chesterton says: 'The offspring of the Missing Link and a mule mated with the child of a manx-cat and a penguin would not outrun the centaur and the griffin, it would merely lack all the interesting features of man and beast and bird: it would not be wilder but much tamer, not fantastic but merely shapeless.'

This stage was indeed reached long ago; even in fairy-tales it is sometimes found (not in good ones). But before we reach it, there is need of renewal and return. We must hark back, to purple and brown, to dragons and centaurs, and so maybe recover camelopards, and green; even (who knows) we may see again yellow, blue, and red, and look upon horses, sheep, and dogs! This recovery fairy-stories help us to make. In that sense only, a taste for them may make (or keep) us childish.

Recovery (which includes return and renewal of health) is a re-gaining—regaining of a clear view. I do not say 'seeing things as they are' and involve myself with the philosophers, though I might venture to say 'seeing things as we are (or were) meant to see them'—as things apart from ourselves. We need, in any case, to clean our windows; so that the things seen clearly may be freed from the drab blur of triteness or familiarity—from possessiveness. Of all faces those of our *familiares* are the ones both most difficult to play fantastic tricks with, and most difficult really to see with fresh attention, perceiving their likeness and unlikeness: that they are faces, and yet unique faces. This triteness is really the penalty of 'appropriation': the things that are trite, or (in a bad sense) familiar, are the things that we have appropriated, legally or mentally. We say we know them. They have become like the things which once attracted us by their glitter, or their colour, or their shape, and we laid hands on them, and then locked them in our hoard, acquired them, and acquiring ceased to look at them.

Of course, fairy-stories are not the only means of recovery, or prophylactic against loss. Humility is enough. And there is (especially for the humble) *Mooreeffoc*, or Chestertonian Fantasy. *Mooreeffoc* is a fantastic word, but it could be seen written up in every town in this land. It is Coffee-room, viewed from the inside through a glass door, as it was seen by Dickens on a dark London day; and it was used by Chesterton to denote the queerness of things that have become trite, when they are seen suddenly from a new angle. That kind of 'fantasy' most people would allow to be wholesome enough; and it can never lack for material. But it has, I think, only a limited power; for the reason that recovery of freshness of vision is its only virtue. The word *Mooreeffoc* may cause you suddenly to realize that England is an utterly alien land, lost either in some remote past age glimpsed by history, or in some strange dim future to be reached only by a time-machine; to see the amazing oddity and interest of its inhabitants and their customs and feeding-habits; but it cannot do more than that: act as a time-telescope focused on one spot. Creative fantasy, because it is mainly trying to do something else (make something new), may open your hoard and let all the locked things fly away like cage-birds. The gems all turn into flowers or flames, and you will be warned that all you had (or knew) was dangerous and potent, not really effectively chained, free and wild; no more yours than they were you.

The 'fantastic' elements in verse and prose of other kinds, even when only decorative or occasional, help in this release. But not so thoroughly as a fairy-story, a thing built on or about Fantasy, of which Fantasy is the core. Fantasy is made out of the Primary World, but a good craftsman loves his material, and has a knowledge and feeling for clay, stone, and wood which only the art of making can give. By the forging of Gram cold iron was revealed; by the making of Pegasus horses were ennobled; in the Trees of the Sun and Moon root and stock, flower and fruit are manifested in glory.

And actually fairy-stories deal largely, or (the better ones) mainly, with simple or fundamental things, untouched by Fantasy, but these simplicities are made all the more luminous by their setting. For the story-maker who allows himself to be 'free with' Nature can be her lover not her slave. It was in fairy-stories that I first divined the potency of the words, and the wonder of the things, such as stone, and wood, and iron; tree and grass; house and fire; bread and wine.

I will now conclude by considering Escape and Consolation, which are naturally closely connected. Though fairy-stories are of course by no means the only medium of Escape, they are to-day one of the most obvious and (to some) outrageous forms of 'escapist' literature; and it is thus reasonable to attach to a consideration of them some consideration of this term 'escape' in criticism generally.

I have claimed that Escape is one of the main functions of fairy-stories, and since I do not disapprove of them, it is plain that I do not accept the tone of scorn or pity with which 'Escape'

is now so often used: a tone for which the uses of the word outside literary criticism give no warrant at all. In what the
misusers of Escape are fond of calling Real Life, Escape is
evidently as a rule very practical, and may even be heroic. In
real life it is difficult to blame it, unless it fails; in criticism it
would seem to be the worse the better it succeeds. Evidently
we are faced by a misuse of words, and also by a confusion of
thought. Why should a man be scorned, if, finding himself in
prison, he tries to get out and go home? Or if, when he cannot
do so, he thinks and talks about other topics than jailers and
prison-walls? The world outside has not become less real
because the prisoner cannot see it. In using Escape in this way
the critics have chosen the wrong word, and, what is more, they
are confusing, not always by sincere error, the Escape of the
Prisoner with the Flight of the Deserter. Just so a Party-
spokesman might have labelled departure from the misery of
the Fuehrer's or any other Reich and even criticism of it as
treachery. In the same way these critics, to make confusion
worse, and so to bring into contempt their opponents, stick
their label of scorn not only on to Desertion, but on to real
Escape, and what are often its companions, Disgust, Anger,
Condemnation, and Revolt. Not only do they confound the
escape of the prisoner with the flight of the deserter; but they
would seem to prefer the acquiescence of the 'quisling' to the
resistance of the patriot. To such thinking you have only to say
'the land you loved is doomed' to excuse any treachery, indeed
to glorify it.

For a trifling instance: not to mention (indeed not to parade)
electric street-lamps of mass-produced pattern in your tale is
Escape (in that sense). But it may, almost certainly does, proceed from a considered disgust for so typical a product of the
Robot Age, that combines elaboration and ingenuity of means
with ugliness, and (often) with inferiority of result. These lamps
may be excluded from the tale simply because they are bad
lamps; and it is possible that one of the lessons to be learnt from
the story is the realization of this fact. But out comes the big
stick: 'Electric lamps have come to stay', they say. Long ago
Chesterton truly remarked that, as soon as he heard that anything 'had come to stay', he knew that it would be very soon
replaced—indeed regarded as pitiably obsolete and shabby.
'The march of Science, its tempo quickened by the needs of war,

goes inexorably on . . . making some things obsolete, and fore-shadowing new developments in the utilization of electricity': an advertisement. This says the same thing only more mena-cingly. The electric street-lamp may indeed be ignored, simply because it is so insignificant and transient. Fairy-stories, at any rate, have many more permanent and fundamental things to talk about. Lightning, for example. The escapist is not so sub-servient to the whims of evanescent fashion as these opponents. He does not make things (which it may be quite rational to regard as bad) his masters or his gods by worshipping them as inevitable, even 'inexorable'. And his opponents, so easily contemptuous, have no guarantee that he will stop there: he might rouse men to pull down the street-lamps. Escapism has another and even wickeder face: Reaction.

Not long ago—incredible though it may seem—I heard a clerk of Oxenford declare that he 'welcomed' the proximity of mass-production robot factories, and the roar of self-obstructive mechanical traffic, because it brought his university into 'con-tact with real life'. He may have meant that the way men were living and working in the twentieth century was increasing in barbarity at an alarming rate, and that the loud demonstration of this in the streets of Oxford might serve as a warning that it is not possible to preserve for long an oasis of sanity in a desert of unreason by mere fences, without actual offensive action (practical and intellectual). I fear he did not. In any case the expression 'real life' in this context seems to fall short of aca-demic standards. The notion that motor-cars are more 'alive' than, say, centaurs or dragons is curious; that they are more 'real' than, say, horses is pathetically absurd. How real, how startlingly alive is a factory chimney compared with an elm-tree: poor obsolete thing, insubstantial dream of an escapist!

For my part, I cannot convince myself that the roof of Bletchley station is more 'real' than the clouds. And as an artefact I find it less inspiring than the legendary dome of heaven. The bridge to platform 4 is to me less interesting than Bifröst guarded by Heimdall with the Gjallarhorn. From the wildness of my heart I cannot exclude the question whether railway-engineers, if they had been brought up on more fantasy, might not have done better with all their abundant means than they commonly do. Fairy-stories might be, I guess, better Masters of Arts than the academic person I have referred to.

Much that he (I must suppose) and others (certainly) would call 'serious' literature is no more than play under a glass roof by the side of a municipal swimming-bath. Fairy-stories may invent monsters that fly the air or dwell in the deep, but at least they do not try to escape from heaven or the sea.

And if we leave aside for a moment 'fantasy', I do not think that the reader or the maker of fairy-stories need even be ashamed of the 'escape' of archaism: of preferring not dragons but horses, castles, sailing-ships, bows and arrows; not only elves, but knights and kings and priests. For it is after all possible for a rational man, after reflection (quite unconnected with fairy-story or romance), to arrive at the condemnation, implicit at least in the mere silence of 'escapist' literature, of progressive things like factories, or the machine-guns and bombs that appear to be their most natural and inevitable, dare we say 'inexorable', products.

'The rawness and ugliness of modern European life'—that real life whose contact we should welcome—'is the sign of a biological inferiority, of an insufficient or false reaction to environment.'[1] The maddest castle that ever came out of a giant's bag in a wild Gaelic story is not only much less ugly than a robot-factory, it is also (to use a very modern phrase) 'in a very real sense' a great deal more real. Why should we not escape from or condemn the 'grim Assyrian' absurdity of top-hats, or the Morlockian horror of factories? They are condemned even by the writers of that most escapist form of all literature, stories of 'Scientifiction'. These prophets often foretell (and many seem to yearn for) a world like one big glass-roofed railway-station. But from them it is as a rule very hard to gather what men in such a world-town will *do*. They may abandon the 'full Victorian panoply' for loose garments (with zip-fasteners), but will use this freedom mainly, it would

[1] Christopher Dawson, *Progress and Religion*, pp. 58, 59. Later he adds: 'Why is the stockbroker less beautiful than an Homeric warrior or an Egyptian priest? Because he is less incorporated with life: he is not inevitable but accidental. . . . The full Victorian panoply of top-hat and frock-coat undoubtedly expressed something essential in the nineteenth-century culture, and hence it has with that culture spread all over the world, as no fashion of clothing has ever done before. It is possible that our descendants will recognize in it a kind of grim Assyrian beauty, fit emblem of the ruthless and great age that created it; but however that may be, it misses the direct and inevitable beauty that all clothing should have, because like its parent culture it was out of touch with the life of nature and of human nature as well.'

appear, in order to play with mechanical toys in the soon-cloying game of moving at high speed. To judge by some of these tales they will still be as lustful, vengeful, and greedy as ever; and the ideals of their idealists hardly reach farther than the splendid notion of building more towns of the same sort on other planets. It is indeed an age of 'improved means to deteriorated ends'. It is part of the essential malady of such days —producing the desire to escape, not indeed from life, but from our present time and self-made misery—that we are acutely conscious both of the ugliness of our works, and of their evil. So that to us evil and ugliness seem indissolubly allied. We find it difficult to conceive of evil and beauty together. The fear of the beautiful fay that ran through the elder ages almost eludes our grasp. Even more alarming: goodness is itself bereft of its proper beauty. In Faërie one can indeed conceive of an ogre who possesses a castle hideous as a nightmare (for the evil of the ogre wills it so), but one cannot conceive of a house built with a good purpose—an inn, a hostel for travellers, the hall of a virtuous and noble king—that is yet sickeningly ugly. At the present day it would be rash to hope to see one that was not—unless it was built before our time.

This, however, is the modern and special (or accidental) 'escapist' aspect of fairy-stories, which they share with romances, and other stories out of or about the past. Many stories out of the past have only become 'escapist' in their appeal through surviving from a time when men were as a rule delighted with the work of their hands into our time when many men feel disgust with man-made things.

But there are also other and more profound 'escapisms' that have always appeared in fairy-tale and legend. There are other things more grim and terrible to fly from than the noise, stench, ruthlessness, and aimlessness of the internal-combustion engine. There are hunger, thirst, poverty, pain, sorrow, injustice, death. And even when men are not facing hard things such as these, there are ancient limitations from which fairy-stories offer a sort of escape, and old ambitions and desires (touching the very roots of fantasy) to which they offer a kind of satisfaction and consolation. Some are pardonable weaknesses or curiosities: such as the desire to visit, free as a fish, the deep sea; or the longing for the noiseless, gracious, economical flight of a bird, that longing which the aeroplane cheats, except in rare moments,

seen high and by wind and distance noiseless, turning in the
sun: that is, precisely when imagined and not used. There are
profounder wishes: such as the desire to converse with other
living things. On this desire, as ancient as the Fall, is largely
founded the talking of beasts and creatures in fairy-tales, and
especially the magical understanding of their proper speech.
This is the root, and not the 'confusion' attributed to the minds
of men of the unrecorded past, an alleged 'absence of the
sense of separation of ourselves from beasts'.[1] A vivid sense
of that separation is very ancient: but also a sense that it was
a severance: a strange fate and a guilt lies on us. Other creatures are like other realms with which Man has broken off
relations, and sees now only from the outside at a distance,
being at war with them, or on the terms of an uneasy armistice.
There are a few men who are privileged to travel abroad a
little; others must be content with travellers' tales. Even about
frogs. In speaking of that rather odd but widespread fairy-
story *The Frog-King* Max Müller asked in his prim way: 'How
came such a story ever to be invented? Human beings were,
we may hope, at all times sufficiently enlightened to know that
a marriage between a frog and the daughter of a queen was
absurd.' Indeed we may hope so! For if not, there would be
no point in this story at all, depending as it does essentially on
the sense of the absurdity. Folk-lore origins (or guesses about
them) are here quite beside the point. It is of little avail to
consider totemism. For certainly, whatever customs or beliefs
about frogs and wells lie behind this story, the frog-shape was
and is preserved in the fairy-story[2] precisely because it was so
queer and the marriage absurd, indeed abominable. Though,
of course, in the versions which concern us, Gaelic, German,
English,[3] there is in fact no wedding between a princess and a
frog: the frog was an enchanted prince. And the point of the
story lies not in thinking frogs possible mates, but in the
necessity of keeping promises (even those with intolerable con-
sequences) that, together with observing prohibitions, runs
through all Fairyland. This is one of the notes of the horns of
Elfland, and not a dim note.

And lastly there is the oldest and deepest desire, the Great

[1] See Note G at end (p. 88).   [2] Or group of similar stories.
[3] *The Queen who sought drink from a certain Well and the Lorgann* (Campbell, xxiii);
Der Froschkönig; *The Maid and the Frog*.

Escape: the Escape from Death. Fairy-stories provide many examples and modes of this—which might be called the genuine *escapist*, or (I would say) *fugitive* spirit. But so do other stories (notably those of scientific inspiration), and so do other studies. Fairy-stories are made by men not by fairies. The human stories of the elves are doubtless full of the Escape from Deathlessness. But our stories cannot be expected always to rise above our common level. They often do. Few lessons are taught more clearly in them than the burden of that kind of immortality, or rather endless serial living, to which the 'fugitive' would fly. For the fairy-story is specially apt to teach such things, of old and still to-day. Death is the theme that most inspired George MacDonald.

But the 'consolation' of fairy-stories has another aspect than the imaginative satisfaction of ancient desires. Far more important is the Consolation of the Happy Ending. Almost I would venture to assert that all complete fairy-stories must have it. At least I would say that Tragedy is the true form of Drama, its highest function; but the opposite is true of Fairy-story. Since we do not appear to possess a word that expresses this opposite—I will call it *Eucatastrophe*. The *eucatastrophic* tale is the true form of fairy-tale, and its highest function.

The consolation of fairy-stories, the joy of the happy ending: or more correctly of the good catastrophe, the sudden joyous 'turn' (for there is no true end to any fairy-tale):[1] this joy, which is one of the things which fairy-stories can produce supremely well, is not essentially 'escapist', nor 'fugitive'. In its fairy-tale—or otherworld—setting, it is a sudden and miraculous grace: never to be counted on to recur. It does not deny the existence of *dyscatastrophe*, of sorrow and failure: the possibility of these is necessary to the joy of deliverance; it denies (in the face of much evidence, if you will) universal final defeat and in so far is *evangelium*, giving a fleeting glimpse of Joy, Joy beyond the walls of the world, poignant as grief.

It is the mark of a good fairy-story, of the higher or more complete kind, that however wild its events, however fantastic or terrible the adventures, it can give to child or man that hears it, when the 'turn' comes, a catch of the breath, a beat and lifting of the heart, near to (or indeed accompanied by) tears, as keen as that given by any form of literary art, and having a peculiar quality.

[1] See Note H at end (p. 89).

Even modern fairy-stories can produce this effect sometimes. It is not an easy thing to do; it depends on the whole story which is the setting of the turn, and yet it reflects a glory backwards. A tale that in any measure succeeds in this point has not wholly failed, whatever flaws it may possess, and whatever mixture or confusion of purpose. It happens even in Andrew Lang's own fairy-story, *Prince Prigio*, unsatisfactory in many ways as that is. When 'each knight came alive and lifted his sword and shouted "long live Prince Prigio"', the joy has a little of that strange mythical fairy-story quality, greater than the event described. It would have none in Lang's tale, if the event described were not a piece of more serious fairy-story 'fantasy' than the main bulk of the story, which ·is in general more frivolous, having the half-mocking smile of the courtly, sophisticated *Conte*.[1] Far more powerful and poignant is the effect in a serious tale of Faërie.[2] In such stories when the sudden 'turn' comes we get a piercing glimpse of joy, and heart's desire, that for a moment passes outside the frame, rends indeed the very web of story, and lets a gleam come through.

> Seven long years I served for thee,
> The glassy hill I clamb for thee,
> The bluidy shirt I wrang for thee,
> And wilt thou not wauken and turn to me?

He heard and turned to her.[3]

Epilogue

This 'joy' which I have selected as the mark of the true fairy-story (or romance), or as the seal upon it, merits more consideration.

Probably every writer making a secondary world, a fantasy, every sub-creator, wishes in some measure to be a real maker, or hopes that he is drawing on reality: hopes that the peculiar quality of this secondary world (if not all the details)[4] are

---

[1] This is characteristic of Lang's wavering balance. On the surface the story is a follower of the 'courtly' French *conte* with a satiric twist, and of Thackeray's *Rose and the Ring* in particular—a kind which being superficial, even frivolous, by nature, does not produce or aim at producing anything so profound; but underneath lies the deeper spirit of the romantic Lang.

[2] Of the kind which Lang called 'traditional', and really preferred.

[3] *The Black Bull of Norroway.*

[4] For all the details may not be 'true': it is seldom that the 'inspiration' is so strong and lasting that it leavens all the lump, and does not leave much that is mere uninspired 'invention'.

derived from Reality, or are flowing into it. If he indeed achieves a quality that can fairly be described by the dictionary definition: 'inner consistency of reality', it is difficult to conceive how this can be, if the work does not in some way partake of reality. The peculiar quality of the 'joy' in successful Fantasy can thus be explained as a sudden glimpse of the underlying reality or truth. It is not only a 'consolation' for the sorrow of this world, but a satisfaction, and an answer to that question 'Is it true?' The answer to this question that I gave at first was (quite rightly): 'If you have built your little world well, yes: it is true in that world.' That is enough for the artist (or the artist part of the artist). But in the 'eucatastrophe' we see in a brief vision that the answer may be greater—it may be a far-off gleam or echo of *evangelium* in the real world. The use of this word gives a hint of my epilogue. It is a serious and dangerous matter. I am a Christian, and so at least should not be suspected of wilful irreverence. Knowing my own ignorance and dullness, it is perhaps presumptuous of me to touch upon such a theme; but if by grace what I say has in any respect any validity, it is, of course, only one facet of a truth incalculably rich: finite only because the capacity of Man for whom this was done is finite.

I would venture to say that approaching the Christian Story from this direction, it has long been my feeling (a joyous feeling) that God redeemed the corrupt making-creatures, men, in a way fitting to this aspect, as to others, of their strange nature. The Gospels contain a fairy-story, or a story of a larger kind which embraces all the essence of fairy-stories. They contain many marvels—peculiarly artistic,[1] beautiful, and moving: 'mythical' in their perfect, self-contained significance; and at the same time powerfully symbolic and allegorical; and among the marvels is the greatest and most complete conceivable eucatastrophe. The Birth of Christ is the eucatastrophe of Man's history. The Resurrection is the eucatastrophe of the story of the Incarnation. This story begins and ends in joy. It has pre-eminently the 'inner consistency of reality'. There is no tale ever told that men would rather find was true, and none

---

[1] The Gospels are not artistic in themselves; the Art is here in the story itself, not in the telling. For the Author of the story was not the evangelists. 'Even the world itself could not contain the books that should be written', if that story had been fully written down.

which so many sceptical men have accepted as true on its own merits. For the Art of it has the supremely convincing tone of Primary Art, that is, of Creation. To reject it leads either to sadness or to wrath.

It is not difficult to imagine the peculiar excitement and joy that one would feel, if any specially beautiful fairy-story were found to be 'primarily' true, its narrative to be history, without thereby necessarily losing the mythical or allegorical significance that it had possessed. It is not difficult, for one is not called upon to try and conceive anything of a quality unknown. The joy would have exactly the same quality, if not the same degree, as the joy which the 'turn' in a fairy-story gives: such joy has the very taste of primary truth. (Otherwise its name would not be joy.) It looks forward (or backward: the direction in this regard is unimportant) to the Great Eucatastrophe. The Christian joy, the *Gloria*, is of the same kind; but it is pre-eminently (infinitely, if our capacity were not finite) high and joyous. Because this story is supreme; and it is true. Art has been verified. God is the Lord, of angels, and of men—and of elves. Legend and History have met and fused.

But in God's kingdom the presence of the greatest does not depress the small. Redeemed Man is still man. Story, fantasy, still go on, and should go on. The Evangelium has not abrogated legends; it has hallowed them, especially the 'happy ending'. The Christian has still to work, with mind as well as body, to suffer, hope, and die; but he may now perceive that all his bents and faculties have a purpose, which can be redeemed. So great is the bounty with which he has been treated that he may now, perhaps, fairly dare to guess that in Fantasy he may actually assist in the effoliation and multiple enrichment of creation. All tales may come true; and yet, at the last, redeemed, they may be as like and as unlike the forms that we give them as Man, finally redeemed, will be like and unlike the fallen that we know.

NOTES

A (p. 45)

The very root (not only the use) of their 'marvels' is satiric, a mockery of unreason; and the 'dream' element is not a mere machinery of introduction and ending, but inherent in the action and transitions. These things children can perceive and appreciate, if left to themselves. But to many, as it was to me, *Alice* is presented as a fairy-story and while this misunderstanding lasts, the distaste for the dream-machinery is felt. There is no suggestion of dream in *The Wind in the Willows*. 'The Mole had been working very hard all the morning, spring-cleaning his little house.' So it begins, and that correct tone is maintained. It is all the more remarkable that A. A. Milne, so great an admirer of this excellent book, should have prefaced to his dramatized version a 'whimsical' opening in which a child is seen telephoning with a daffodil. Or perhaps it is not very remarkable, for a perceptive admirer (as distinct from a great admirer) of the book would never have attempted to dramatize it. Naturally only the simpler ingredients, the pantomime, and the satiric beast-fable elements, are capable of presentation in this form. The play is, on the lower level of drama, tolerably good fun, especially for those who have not read the book; but some children that I took to see *Toad of Toad Hall*, brought away as their chief memory nausea at the opening. For the rest they preferred their recollections of the book.

B (p. 57)

Of course, these details, as a rule, got into the tales, *even in the days when they were real practices*, because they had a story-making value. If I were to write a story in which it happened that a man was hanged, that *might* show in later ages, if the story survived—in itself a sign that the story possessed some permanent, and more than local or temporary, value—that it was written at a period when men were really hanged, as a legal practice. *Might*: the inference would not, of course, in that future time be certain. For certainty on that point the future inquirer would have to know definitely when hanging was practised and when I lived. I could have borrowed the incident from other times and places, from other stories; I could simply have invented it. But even if this inference happened to be correct, the hanging-scene would only occur in the story, (*a*) because I was aware of the dramatic, tragic, or macabre force of this incident in my tale, and (*b*) because those who handed it down felt this force enough to make them keep the incident in. Distance of time, sheer antiquity and alienness, might later sharpen the edge of the tragedy or the horror; but the edge must be there even for the elvish hone of antiquity to whet it. The least useful question, therefore, for literary critics at any rate, to ask or to answer about Iphigeneia, daughter of Agamemnon, is: Does the legend of her sacrifice at Aulis come down from a time when human-sacrifice was commonly practised?

I say only 'as a rule', because it is conceivable that what is now regarded as a 'story' was once something different in intent: e.g. a record of fact or ritual. I mean 'record' strictly. A story invented to explain a ritual (a process that is sometimes supposed to have frequently occurred) remains primarily a story. It takes form as such, and will survive (long after the ritual evidently) only because of its story-values. In some cases details that now are notable merely because they are strange may have once been so everyday and unregarded that they were slipped in casually: like mentioning that a man 'raised his hat', or 'caught a train'. But such casual details will not long survive change in everyday habits. Not in a period of oral transmission. In a period of writing (and of rapid changes in habits) a story may remain unchanged long enough for even its casual details to acquire the value of quaintness or queerness. Much of Dickens now has this air. One can open to-day an edition of a novel of his that was bought and first read when things were so in everyday life as they are in the story, though these everyday details are now already as remote from our daily habits as the Elizabethan period. But that is a special modern situation. The anthropologists and folk-lorists do not imagine any conditions of that kind. But if they are dealing with unlettered oral transmission, then they should all the more reflect that in that case they are dealing with items whose primary object was story-building, and whose primary reason for survival was the same. The Frog-King (see p. 80) is not a *Credo*, nor a manual of totem-law: it is a queer tale with a plain moral.

C (p. 59)

As far as my knowledge goes, children who have an early bent for writing have no special inclination to attempt the writing of fairy-stories, unless that has been almost the sole form of literature presented to them; and they fail most markedly when they try. It is not an easy form. If children have any special leaning it is to Beast-fable, which adults often confuse with Fairy-story. The best stories by children that I have seen have been either 'realistic' (in intent), or have had as their characters animals and birds, who were in the main the zoomorphic human beings usual in Beast-fable. I imagine that this form is so often adopted principally because it allows a large measure of realism: the representation of domestic events and talk that children really know. The form itself is, however, as a rule, suggested or imposed by adults. It has a curious preponderance in the literature, good and bad, that is nowadays commonly presented to young children: I suppose it is felt to go with 'Natural History', semi-scientific books about beasts and birds that are also considered to be proper pabulum for the young. And it is reinforced by the bears and rabbits that seem in recent times almost to have ousted human dolls from the play-rooms even of little girls. Children make up sagas, often long and elaborate, about their dolls. If these are shaped like bears, bears will be the characters of the sagas; but they will talk like people.

D (p. 63)

I was introduced to zoology and palaeontology ('for children') quite as early as to Faërie. I saw pictures of living beasts and of true (so I was told) prehistoric animals. I liked the 'prehistoric' animals best: they had at least lived long ago, and hypothesis (based on somewhat slender evidence) cannot avoid a gleam of fantasy. But I did not like being told that these creatures were 'dragons'. I can still re-feel the irritation that I felt in childhood at assertions of instructive relatives (or their gift-books) such as these: 'snow-flakes are fairy jewels', or 'are more beautiful than fairy jewels'; 'the marvels of the ocean depths are more wonderful than fairyland'. Children expect the differences they feel but cannot analyse to be explained by their elders, or at least recognized, not to be ignored or denied. I was keenly alive to the beauty of 'Real things', but it seemed to me quibbling to confuse this with the wonder of 'Other things'. I was eager to study Nature, actually more eager than I was to read most fairy-stories; but I did not want to be quibbled into Science and cheated out of Faërie by people who seemed to assume that by some kind of original sin I should prefer fairy-tales, but according to some kind of new religion I ought to be induced to like science. Nature is no doubt a life-study, or a study for eternity (for those so gifted); but there is a part of man which is not 'Nature', and which therefore is not obliged to study it, and is, in fact, wholly unsatisfied by it.

E (p. 68)

There is, for example, in surrealism commonly present a morbidity or un-ease very rarely found in literary fantasy. The mind that produced the depicted images may often be suspected to have been in fact already morbid; yet this is not a necessary explanation in all cases. A curious disturbance of the mind is often set up by the very act of drawing things of this kind, a state similar in quality and consciousness of morbidity to the sensations in a high fever, when the mind develops a distressing fecundity and facility in figure-making, seeing forms sinister or grotesque in all visible objects about it.

I am speaking here, of course, of the primary expression of Fantasy in 'pictorial' arts, not of 'illustrations'; nor of the cinematograph. However good in themselves, illustrations do little good to fairy-stories. The radical distinction between all art (including drama) that offers a *visible* presentation and true literature is that it imposes one visible form. Literature works from mind to mind and is thus more progenitive. It is at once more universal and more poignantly particular. If it speaks of *bread* or *wine* or *stone* or *tree*, it appeals to the whole of these things, to their ideas; yet each hearer will give to them a peculiar personal embodiment in his imagination. Should the story say 'he ate bread', the dramatic producer or painter can only show 'a piece of bread' according to his taste or fancy, but the hearer of the story will think of bread in general and picture it in some form of his own. If a story says 'he climbed a hill and saw a river in the valley below', the illustrator may catch, or nearly catch, his own vision of such a scene; but every hearer of the words will have his own picture, and it will be made out of all the hills and rivers and dales he has ever seen, but specially out of The Hill, The River, The Valley which were for him the first embodiment of the word.

F (p. 69)

I am referring, of course, primarily to fantasy of forms and visible shapes. Drama can be made out of the impact upon human characters of some event of Fantasy, or Faërie, that requires no machinery, or that can be assumed or reported to have happened. But that is not fantasy in dramatic result; the human characters hold the stage and upon them attention is concentrated. Drama of this sort (exemplified by some of Barrie's plays) can be used frivolously, or it can be used for satire, or for conveying such 'messages' as the playwright may have in his mind—for men. Drama is anthropocentric. Fairy-story and Fantasy need not be. There are, for instance, many stories telling how men and women have disappeared and spent years among the fairies, without noticing the passage of time, or appearing to grow older. In *Mary Rose* Barrie wrote a play on this theme. No fairy is seen. The cruelly tormented human beings are there all the time. In spite of the sentimental star and the angelic voices at the end (in the printed version) it is a painful play, and can easily be made diabolic: by substituting (as I have seen it done) the elvish call for 'angel voices' at the end. The non-dramatic fairy-stories, in so far as they are concerned with the human victims, can also be pathetic or horrible. But they need not be. In most of them the fairies are also there, on equal terms. In some stories they are the real interest. Many of the short folk-lore accounts of such incidents purport to be just pieces of 'evidence' about fairies, items in an agelong accumulation of 'lore' concerning them and the modes of their existence. The sufferings of human beings who come into contact with them (often enough, wilfully) are thus seen in quite a different perspective. A drama could be made about the sufferings of a victim of research in radiology, but hardly about radium itself. But it is possible to be primarily interested in radium (not radiologists)—or primarily interested in Faërie, not tortured mortals. One interest will produce a scientific book, the other a fairy-story. Drama cannot well cope with either.

G (p. 80)

The absence of this sense is a mere hypothesis concerning men of the lost past, whatever wild confusions men of to-day, degraded or deluded, may suffer. It is just as legitimate an hypothesis, and one more in agreement with what little is recorded concerning the thoughts of men of old on this subject, that this sense was once stronger. That fantasies which blended the human form with animal and vegetable forms, or gave human faculties to beasts, are ancient is, of course, no evidence for confusion at all. It is, if anything, evidence to the contrary. Fantasy does not blur the sharp outlines of the real world; for it depends on them. As far as our western, European, world is concerned, this 'sense of separation' has in fact been attacked and weakened in modern times not by fantasy but by scientific theory. Not by stories of centaurs or werewolves or enchanted bears, but by the hypotheses (or dogmatic guesses) of scientific writers who classed Man not only as 'an animal'—that correct classification is ancient—but as 'only an animal'. There has been a consequent distortion of sentiment. The natural love of men not wholly corrupt for beasts, and the human desire to 'get inside the skin' of living things, has run riot. We now get men who love animals more than men; who pity sheep so much that they curse shepherds as wolves; who weep over a slain war-horse and vilify dead soldiers. It is now, not in the days when fairy-stories were begotten, that we get 'an absence of the sense of separation'.

It is a curious result of the application of evolutionary hypothesis concerning Man's animal body to his whole being, that it tends to produce both arrogance and servility. Man has merely succeeded (it seems) in dominating other animals by force and chicane, not by hereditary right. He is a tyrant not a king. A cat may look at a king; but let no cat look at a tyrant! As for men taking animal form, or animals doing human things, this is dangerous indecent nonsense, insulting to the *Herrenvolk*. But strong or proud men talk of breeding other men like their cattle, and for similar purposes. For a self-chosen *Herrenvolk* always ends by becoming the slaves of a gang, a *Herrenbande*.

H (p. 81)

The verbal ending—usually held to be as typical of the end of fairy-stories as 'once upon a time' is of the beginning—'and they lived happily ever after' is an artificial device. It does not deceive anybody. End-phrases of this kind are to be compared to the margins and frames of pictures, and are no more to be thought of as the real end of any particular fragment of the seamless Web of Story than the frame is of the visionary scene, or the casement of the Outer World. These phrases may be plain or elaborate, simple or extravagant, as artificial and as necessary as frames plain, or carved, or gilded. 'And if they have not gone away they are there still.' 'My story is done—see there is a little mouse; anyone who catches it may make himself a fine fur cap of it.' 'And they lived happily ever after.' 'And when the wedding was over, they sent me home with little paper shoes on a cause-way of pieces of glass.'

Endings of this sort suit fairy-stories, because such tales have a greater sense and grasp of the endlessness of the World of Story than most modern 'realistic' stories, already hemmed within the narrow confines of their own small time. A sharp cut in the endless tapestry is not unfittingly marked by a formula, even a grotesque or comic one. It was an irresistible development of modern illustration (so largely photographic) that borders should be abandoned and the 'picture' end only with the paper. This method may be suitable for photographs; but it is altogether inappropriate for the pictures that illustrate or are inspired by fairy-stories. An enchanted forest requires a margin, even an elaborate border. To print it conterminous with the page, like a 'shot' of the Rockies in 'Picture Post', as if it were indeed a 'snap' of fairyland or a 'sketch by our artist on the spot', is a folly and an abuse.

As for the beginnings of fairy-stories: one can scarcely improve on the formula *Once upon a time*. It has an immediate effect. This effect can be appreciated by reading, for instance, the fairy-story *The Terrible Head* in the *Blue Fairy Book*. It is Andrew Lang's own adaptation of the story of Perseus and the Gorgon. It begins 'once upon a time', and it does not name any year or land or person. Now this treatment does something which could be called 'turning mythology into fairy-story'. I should prefer to say that it turns high fairy-story (for such is the Greek tale) into a particular form that is at present familiar in our land: a nursery or 'old wives' form. Namelessness is not a virtue but an accident, and should not have been imitated; for vagueness in this regard is a debasement, a corruption due to forgetfulness and lack of skill. But not so, I think, the timelessness. That beginning is not poverty-stricken but significant. It produces at a stroke the sense of a great uncharted world of time.

ON STORIES

C. S. LEWIS

IT is astonishing how little attention critics have paid to Story considered in itself. Granted the story, the style in which it should be told, the order in which it should be disposed, and (above all) the delineation of the characters, have been abundantly discussed. But the Story itself, the series of imagined events, is nearly always passed over in silence, or else treated exclusively as affording opportunities for the delineation of character. There are indeed three notable exceptions. Aristotle in the *Poetics* constructed a theory of Greek tragedy which puts Story in the centre and relegates character to a strictly subordinate place. In the Middle Ages and the early Renaissance, Boccaccio and others developed an allegorical theory of Story to explain the ancient myths. And in our own time Jung and his followers have produced their doctrine of Archtypes. Apart from these three attempts the subject has been left almost untouched, and this has had a curious result. Those forms of literature in which Story exists merely as a means to something else—for example, the novel of manners where the story is there for the sake of the characters, or the criticism of social conditions—have had full justice done to them; but those forms in which everything else is there for the sake of the story have been given little serious attention. Not only have they been despised, as if they were fit only for children, but even the kind of pleasure they give has, in my opinion, been misunderstood. It is the second injustice which I am most anxious to remedy. Perhaps the pleasure of Story comes as low in the scale as modern criticism puts it. I do not think so myself, but on that point we may agree to differ. Let us, however, try to see clearly what kind of pleasure it is: or rather, what different kinds of pleasure it may be. For I suspect that a very hasty assumption has been made on this subject. I think that books which are read merely 'for the story' may be enjoyed in two very different ways. It is partly a division of books (some stories can be read only in the one spirit and some only in the other) and partly a division of readers (the same story can be read in different ways).

What finally convinced me of this distinction was a conversation which I had a few years ago with an intelligent American pupil. We were talking about the books which had delighted our boyhood. His favourite had been Fenimore Cooper whom (as it happens) I have never read. My friend described one particular scene in which the hero was half-sleeping by his bivouac fire in the woods while a Redskin with a tomahawk was silently creeping on him from behind. He remembered the breathless excitement with which he had read the passage, the agonized suspense with which he wondered whether the hero would wake up in time or not. But I, remembering the great moments in my own early reading, felt quite sure that my friend was misrepresenting his experience, and indeed leaving out the real point. Surely, surely, I thought, the sheer excitement, the suspense, was not what had kept him going back and back to Fenimore Cooper. If that were what he wanted any other 'boy's blood' would have done as well. I tried to put my thought into words. I asked him whether he were sure that he was not over-emphasizing and falsely isolating the importance of the danger simply as danger. For though I had never read Fenimore Cooper I had enjoyed other books about 'Red Indians'. And I knew that what I wanted from them was not simply 'excitement'. Dangers, of course, there must be: how else can you keep a story going? But they must (in the mood which led one to such a book) be Redskin dangers. The 'Redskin-nery' was what really mattered. In such a scene as my friend had described, take away the feathers, the high cheek-bones, the whiskered trousers, substitute a pistol for a tomahawk, and what would be left? For I wanted not the momentary suspense but that whole world to which it belonged—the snow and the snow-shoes, beavers and canoes, war-paths and wigwams, and Hiawatha names. Thus I; and then came the shock. My pupil is a very clear-headed man and he saw at once what I meant and also saw how totally his imaginative life as a boy had differed from mine. He replied that he was perfectly certain that 'all that' had made no part of his pleasure. He had never cared one brass farthing for it. Indeed—and this really made me feel as if I were talking to a visitor from another planet—in so far as he had been dimly aware of 'all that', he had resented it as a distraction from the main issue. He would, if anything, have preferred to the Redskin some more ordinary danger such as a crook with a revolver.

To those whose literary experiences are at all like my own the distinction which I am trying to make between two kinds of pleasure will probably be clear enough from this one example. But to make it doubly clear I will add another. I was once taken to see a film version of *King Solomon's Mines*. Of its many sins—not least the introduction of a totally irrelevant young woman in shorts who accompanied the three adventurers wherever they went—only one here concerns us. At the end of Haggard's book, as everyone remembers, the heroes are awaiting death entombed in a rock chamber and surrounded by the mummified kings of that land. The maker of the film version, however, apparently thought this tame. He substituted a subterranean volcanic eruption, and then went one better by adding an earthquake. Perhaps we should not blame him. Perhaps the scene in the original was not 'cinematic' and the man was right, by the canons of his own art, in altering it. But it would have been better not to have chosen in the first place a story which could be adapted to the screen only by being ruined. Ruined, at least, for me. No doubt if sheer excitement is all you want from a story, and if increase of dangers increases excitement, then a rapidly changing series of two risks (that of being burned alive and that of being crushed to bits) would be better than the single prolonged danger of starving to death in a cave. But that is just the point. There must be a pleasure in such stories distinct from mere excitement or I should not feel that I had been cheated in being given the earthquake instead of Haggard's actual scene. What I lose is the whole sense of the deathly (quite a different thing from simple danger of death)—the cold, the silence, and the surrounding faces of the ancient, the crowned and sceptred, dead. You may, if you please, say that Rider Haggard's effect is quite as 'crude' or 'vulgar' or 'sensational' as that which the film substituted for it. I am not at present discussing that. The point is that it is extremely different. The one lays a hushing spell on the imagination; the other excites a rapid flutter of the nerves. In reading that chapter of the book curiosity or suspense about the escape of the heroes from their death-trap makes a very minor part of one's experience. The trap I remember for ever: how they got out I have long since forgotten.

It seems to me that in talking of books which are 'mere stories'—books, that is, which concern themselves principally

with the imagined event and not with character or society—
nearly everyone makes the assumption that 'excitement' is the
only pleasure they ever give or are intended to give. *Excitement,* in
this sense, may be defined as the alternate tension and appease-
ment of imagined anxiety. This is what I think untrue. In some
such books, and for some readers, another factor comes in.

To put it at the very lowest, I know that something else
comes in for at least one reader—myself. I must here be autobiographical for the sake of being evidential. Here is a man
who has spent more hours than he cares to remember in reading
romances, and received from them more pleasure perhaps than
he should. I know the geography of Tormance better than that
of Tellus. I have been more curious about travels from Uplands
to Utterbol and from Morna Moruna to Koshtra Belorn than
about those recorded in Hakluyt. Though I saw the trenches
before Arras I could not now lecture on them so tactically as
on the Greek wall, and Scamander and the Scaean Gate. As
a social historian I am sounder on Toad Hall and the Wild
Wood or the cave-dwelling Selenites or Hrothgar's court or
Vortigern's than on London, Oxford, and Belfast. If to love
Story is to love excitement then I ought to be the greatest lover
of excitement alive. But the fact is that what is said to be the most
'exciting' novel in the world, *The Three Musketeers,* makes no
appeal to me at all. The total lack of atmosphere repels me.
There is no country in the book—save as a storehouse of inns
and ambushes. There is no weather. When they cross to
London there is no feeling that London differs from Paris.
There is not a moment's rest from the 'adventures': one's nose
is kept ruthlessly to the grindstone. It all means nothing to me.
If that is what is meant by Romance, then Romance is my
aversion and I greatly prefer George Eliot or Trollope. In
saying this I am not attempting to criticize *The Three Musketeers.*
I believe on the testimony of others that it is a capital story.
I am sure that my own inability to like it is in me a defect and
a misfortune. But that misfortune is evidence. If a man sensi-
tive and perhaps over-sensitive to Romance likes least that
Romance which is, by common consent, the most 'exciting' of
all, then it follows that 'excitement' is not the only kind of
pleasure to be got out of Romance. If a man loves wine and
yet hates one of the strongest wines, then surely the sole source
of pleasure in wine cannot be the alcohol?

If I am alone in this experience then, to be sure, the present essay is of merely autobiographical interest. But I am pretty sure that I am not absolutely alone. I write on the chance that some others may feel the same and in the hope that I may help them to clarify their own sensations.

In the example of *King Solomon's Mines* the producer of the film substituted at the climax one kind of danger for another and thereby, for me, ruined the story. But where excitement is the only thing that matters kinds of danger must be irrelevant. Only degrees of danger will matter. The greater the danger and the narrower the hero's escape from it, the more exciting the story will be. But when we are concerned with the 'something else' this is not so. Different kinds of danger strike different chords from the imagination. Even in real life different kinds of danger produce different kinds of fear. There may come a point at which fear is so great that such distinctions vanish, but that is another matter. There is a fear which is twin sister to awe, such as a man in war-time feels when he first comes within sound of the guns; there is a fear which is twin sister to disgust, such as a man feels on finding a snake or scorpion in his bedroom. There are taut, quivering fears (for one split second hardly distinguishable from a kind of pleasureable thrill) that a man may feel on a dangerous horse or a dangerous sea; and again, dead, squashed, flattened, numbing fears, as when we think we have cancer or cholera. There are also fears which are not of *danger* at all: like the fear of some large and hideous, though innocuous, insect or the fear of a ghost. All this, even in real life. But in imagination, where the fear does not rise to abject terror and is not discharged in action, the qualitative difference is much stronger.

I can never remember a time when it was not, however vaguely, present to my consciousness. *Jack the Giant-Killer* is not, in essence, simply the story of a clever hero surmounting danger. It is in essence the story of such a hero surmounting *danger from giants*. It is quite easy to contrive a story in which, though the enemies are of normal size, the odds against Jack are equally great. But it will be quite a different story. The whole quality of the imaginative response is determined by the fact that the enemies are giants. That heaviness, that monstrosity, that uncouthness, hangs over the whole thing. Turn it into music and you will feel the difference at once. If your villain is a giant your orchestra will proclaim his entrance in one way: if he is any other kind of villain, in another. I have seen landscapes (notably in the Mourne Mountains) which, under a particular light, made me feel that at any moment a giant might raise his head over the next ridge. Nature has that in her which compels us to invent giants: and only giants will do. (Notice that Gawain was in the north-west corner of England when 'etins aneleden him', giants came *blowing* after him on the high fells. Can it be an accident that Wordsworth was in the same places when he heard 'low breathings coming after him'?) The dangerousness of the giants is, though important, secondary. In some folk-tales we meet giants who are not dangerous. But they still affect us in much the same way. A *good* giant is legitimate: but he would be twenty tons of living, earth-shaking oxymoron. The intolerable pressure, the sense of something older, wilder, and more earthy than humanity, would still cleave to him.

But let us descend to a lower instance. Are pirates, any more than giants, merely a machine for threatening the hero? That sail which is rapidly overhauling us may be an ordinary enemy: a Don or a Frenchman. The ordinary enemy may easily be made just as lethal as the pirate. At the moment when she runs up the Jolly Roger, what exactly does this do to the imagination? It means, I grant you, that if we are beaten there will be no quarter. But that could be contrived without piracy. It is not the mere increase of danger that does the trick. It is the whole image of the utterly lawless enemy, the men who have cut adrift from all human society and become, as it were, a species of their own—men strangely clad, dark men with ear-rings, men with a history which they know and we don't, lords of unspecified treasure buried in undiscovered islands. They are, in fact, to the young reader almost as mythological as the giants. It does not cross his mind that a man—a mere man like the rest of us—might be a pirate at one time of his life and not at another, or that there is any smudgy frontier between piracy and privateering. A pirate is a pirate, just as a giant is a giant.

Consider, again, the enormous difference between being shut out and being shut in: if you like between agoraphobia and claustrophobia. In *King Solomon's Mines* the heroes were shut in: so, more terribly, the narrator imagined himself to be in

Poe's *Premature Burial*. Your breath shortens while you read it. Now remember the chapter called 'Mr. Bedford Alone' in H. G. Wells's *First Men in the Moon*. There Bedford finds himself shut out on the surface of the Moon just as the long lunar day is drawing to its close—and with the day go the air and all heat. Read it from the terrible moment when the first tiny snowflake startles him into a realization of his position down to the point at which he reaches the 'sphere' and is saved. Then ask yourself whether what you have been feeling is simply suspense. 'Over me, around me, closing in on me, embracing me ever nearer was the Eternal . . . the infinite and final Night of space.' That is the idea which has kept you enthralled. But if we were concerned only with the question whether Mr. Bedford will live or freeze, that idea is quite beside the purpose. You can die of cold between Russian Poland and new Poland, just as well as by going to the Moon, and the pain will be equal. For the purpose of killing Mr. Bedford 'the infinite and final Night of space' is almost entirely otiose: what is by cosmic standards an infinitesimal change of temperature is sufficient to kill a man and absolute zero can do no more. That airless outer darkness is important not for what it can do to Bedford but for what it does to us: to trouble us with Pascal's old fear of those eternal silences which have gnawed at so much religious faith and shattered so many humanistic hopes: to evoke with them and through them all our racial and childish memories of exclusion and desolation: to present, in fact, as an intuition one permanent aspect of human experience.

And here, I expect, we come to one of the differences between life and art. A man really in Bedford's position would probably not feel very acutely that sidereal loneliness. The immediate issue of death would drive the contemplative object out of his mind: he would have no interest in the many degrees of increasing cold lower than the one which made his survival impossible. That is one of the functions of art: to present what the narrow and desperately practical perspectives of real life exclude.

I have sometimes wondered whether the 'excitement' may not be an element actually hostile to the deeper imagination. In inferior romances, such as the American magazines of 'scientifiction' supply, we often come across a really suggestive idea. But the author has no expedient for keeping the story on the move except that of putting his hero into violent danger.

In the hurry and scurry of his escapes the poetry of the basic idea is lost. In a much milder degree I think this has happened to Wells himself in the *War of the Worlds*. What really matters in this story is the idea of being attacked by something utterly 'outside'. As in *Piers Plowman* destruction has come upon us 'from the planets'. If the Martian invaders are merely dangerous—if we once become mainly concerned with the fact that they can *kill* us—why, then, a burglar or a bacillus can do as much. The real nerve of the romance is laid bare when the hero first goes to look at the newly fallen projectile on Horsell Common. 'The yellowish-white metal that gleamed in the crack between the lid and the cylinder had an unfamiliar hue. *Extra-terrestrial* had no meaning for most of the onlookers.' But *extra-terrestrial* is the key word of the whole story. And in the later horrors, excellently as they are done, we lose the feeling of it. Similarly in the Poet Laureate's *Sard Harker* it is the journey across the Sierras that really matters. That the man who has heard that noise in the cañon—'He could not think what it was. It was not sorrowful nor joyful nor terrible. It was great and strange. It was like the rock speaking'—that this man should be later in danger of mere murder is almost an impertinence.

It is here that Homer shows his supreme excellence. The landing on Circe's island, the sight of the smoke going up from amidst those unexplored woods, the god meeting us ('the messenger, the slayer of Argus')—what an anti-climax if all these had been the prelude only to some ordinary risk of life and limb! But the peril that lurks here, the silent, painless, unendurable change into brutality, is worthy of the setting. Mr. de la Mare too has surmounted the difficulty. The threat launched in the opening paragraphs of his best stories is seldom fulfilled in any identifiable event: still less is it dissipated. Our fears are never, in one sense, realized: yet we lay down the story feeling that they, and far more, were justified. But perhaps the most remarkable achievement in this kind is that of Mr. David Lindsay's *Voyage to Arcturus*. The experienced reader, noting the threats and promises of the opening chapter, even while he gratefully enjoys them, feels sure that they cannot be carried out. He reflects that in stories of this kind the first chapter is nearly always the best and reconciles himself to disappointment; Tormance, when we reach it, he forbodes, will be less interesting

than Tormance seen from the Earth. But never will he have
been more mistaken. Unaided by any special skill or even any
sound taste in language, the author leads us up a stair of unpre-
dictables. In each chapter we think we have found his final
position: each time we are utterly mistaken. He builds whole
worlds of imagery and passion, any one of which would have
served another writer for a whole book, only to pull each of them
to pieces and pour scorn on it. The physical dangers, which are
plentiful, here count for nothing: it is we ourselves and the
author who walk through a world of spiritual dangers which
makes them seem trivial. There is no recipe for writing of this
kind. But part of the secret is that the author (like Kafka) is
recording a lived dialectic. His Tormance is a region of the
spirit. He is the first writer to discover what 'other planets' are
really good for in fiction. No merely physical strangeness or
merely spatial distance will realize that idea of otherness which
is what we are always trying to grasp in a story about voyaging
through space: you must go into another dimension. To con-
struct plausible and moving 'other worlds' you must draw on
the only real 'other world' we know, that of the spirit.

   Notice here the corollary. If some fatal progress of applied
science ever enables us in fact to reach the Moon, that real
journey will not at all satisfy the impulse which we now seek to
gratify by writing such stories. The real Moon, if you could
reach it and survive, would in a deep and deadly sense be just
like anywhere else. You would find cold, hunger, hardship,
and danger; and after the first few hours they would be *simply*
cold, hunger, hardship, and danger as you might have met
them on Earth. And death would be simply death among
those bleached craters as it is simply death in a nursing home at
Sheffield. No man would find an abiding strangeness on the
Moon unless he were the sort of man who could find it in his
own back garden. 'He who would bring home the wealth of
the Indies must carry the wealth of the Indies with him.'

   Good stories often introduce the marvellous or supernatural,
and nothing about Story has been so often misunderstood as
this. Thus, for example, Dr. Johnson, if I remember rightly,
thought that children liked stories of the marvellous because
they were too ignorant to know that they were impossible. But
children do not always like them, nor are those who like them
always children; and to enjoy reading about fairies—much

more about giants and dragons—it is not necessary to believe in them. Belief is at best irrelevant; it may be a positive disadvantage. Nor are the marvels in good Story ever mere arbitrary fictions stuck on to make the narrative more sensational. I happened to remark to a man who was sitting beside me at dinner the other night that I was reading Grimm in German of an evening but never bothered to look up a word I didn't know, 'so that it is often great fun' (I added) 'guessing what it was that the old woman gave to the prince which he afterwards lost in the wood'. 'And specially difficult in a fairytale,' said he, 'where everything is arbitrary and therefore the object might be anything at all.' His error was profound. The logic of a fairy-tale is as strict as that of a realistic novel, though different.

Does anyone believe that Kenneth Grahame made an arbitrary choice when he gave his principal character the form of a toad, or that a stag, a pigeon, a lion would have done as well? The choice is based on the fact that the real toad's face has a grotesque resemblance to a certain kind of human face— a rather apoplectic face with a fatuous grin on it. This is, no doubt, an accident in the sense that all the lines which suggest the resemblance are really there for quite different biological reasons. The ludicrous quasi-human expression is therefore changeless: the toad cannot stop grinning because its 'grin' is not really a grin at all. Looking at the creature we thus see, isolated and fixed, an aspect of human vanity in its funniest and most pardonable form; following that hint Grahame creates Mr. Toad—an ultra-Jonsonian 'humour'. And we bring back the wealth of the Indies; we have henceforward more amusement in, and kindness towards, a certain kind of vanity in real life.

But why should the characters be disguised as animals at all? The disguise is very thin, so thin that Grahame makes Mr. Toad on one occasion 'comb the dry leaves out of his *hair*'. Yet it is quite indispensable. If you try to rewrite the book with all the characters humanized you are faced at the outset with a dilemma. Are they to be adults or children? You will find that they can be neither. They are like children in so far as they have no responsibilities, no struggle for existence, no domestic cares. Meals turn up; one does not even ask who cooked them. In Mr. Badger's kitchen 'plates on the dresser grinned at pots on the shelf'. Who kept them clean? Where were they bought? How were they delivered in the Wild Wood? Mole is very snug in his subterranean home, but what was he living *on*? If he is a *rentier* where is the bank, what are his investments? The tables in his forecourt were 'marked with rings that hinted at beer mugs'. But where did he get the beer? In that way the life of all the characters is that of children for whom everything is provided and who take everything for granted. But in other ways it is the life of adults. They go where they like and do what they please, they arrange their own lives.

To that extent the book is a specimen of the most scandalous escapism: it paints a happiness under incompatible conditions —the sort of freedom we can have only in childhood and the sort we can have only in maturity—and conceals the contradiction by the further pretence that the characters are not human beings at all. The one absurdity helps to hide the other. It might be expected that such a book would unfit us for the harshness of reality and send us back to our daily lives unsettled and discontented. I do not find that it does so. The happiness which it presents to us is in fact full of the simplest and most attainable things—food, sleep, exercise, friendship, the face of nature, even (in a sense) religion. That 'simple but sustaining meal' of 'bacon and broad beans and a macaroni pudding' which Rat gave to his friends has, I doubt not, helped down many a real nursery dinner. And in the same way the whole story, paradoxically enough, strengthens our relish for real life. This excursion into the preposterous sends us back with renewed pleasure to the actual.

It is usual to speak in a playfully apologetic tone about one's adult enjoyment of what are called 'children's books'. I think the convention a silly one. No book is really worth reading at the age of ten which is not equally (and often far more) worth reading at the age of fifty—except, of course, books of information. The only imaginative works we ought to grow out of are those which it would have been better not to have read at all. A mature palate will probably not much care for *crème de menthe*: but it ought still to enjoy bread and butter and honey.

Another very large class of stories turns on fulfilled prophecies—the story of Oedipus, or *The Man who would be King*, or *The Hobbit*. In most of them the very steps taken to prevent the fulfilment of the prophecy actually bring it about. It is foretold that Oedipus will kill his father and marry his mother. In order to prevent this from happening he is exposed on the mountain: and that exposure, by leading to his rescue and thus to his life among strangers in ignorance of his real parentage, renders possible both the disasters. Such stories produce (at least in me) a feeling of awe, coupled with a certain sort of bewilderment such as one often feels in looking at a complex pattern of lines that pass over and under one another. One sees, yet does not quite see, the regularity. And is there not good occasion both for awe and bewilderment? We have just had set before our imagination something that has always baffled the intellect: we have *seen* how destiny and free will can be combined, even how free will is the *modus operandi* of destiny. The story does what no theorem can quite do. It may not be 'like real life' in the superficial sense: but it sets before us an image of what reality may well be like at some more central region.

It will be seen that throughout this essay I have taken my examples indiscriminately from books which critics would (quite rightly) place in very different categories—from American 'scientifiction' and Homer, from Sophocles and *Märchen*, from children's stories and the intensely sophisticated art of Mr. de la Mare. This does not mean that I think them of equal literary merit. But if I am right in thinking that there is another enjoyment in Story besides the excitement, then popular romance even on the lowest level becomes rather more important than we had supposed. When you see an immature or uneducated person devouring what seem to you merely sensational stories, can you be sure what kind of pleasure he is enjoying? It is, of course, no good asking *him*. If he were capable of analysing his own experience as the question requires him to do, he would be neither uneducated nor immature. But because he is inarticulate we must not give judgement against him. He may be seeking only the recurring tension of imagined anxiety. But he may also, I believe, be receiving certain profound experiences which are, for him, not acceptable in any other form.

Mr. Roger Green, writing in *English* not long ago, remarked that the reading of Rider Haggard had been to many a sort of religious experience. To some people this will have seemed simply grotesque. I myself would strongly disagree with it if 'religious' is taken to mean 'Christian'. And even if we take it in a sub-Christian sense, it would have been safer to say that such people had first met in Haggard's romances elements which they would meet again in religious experience if they ever came to have any. But I think Mr. Green is very much nearer the mark than those who assume that no one has ever read the romances except in order to be thrilled by hair-breadth escapes. If he had said simply that something which the educated receive from poetry can reach the masses through stories of adventure, and almost in no other way, then I think he would have been right. If so, nothing can be more disastrous than the view that the cinema can and should replace popular written fiction. The elements which it excludes are precisely those which give the untrained mind its only access to the imaginative world. There is death in the camera.

As I have admitted, it is very difficult to tell in any given case whether a story is piercing to the unliterary reader's deeper imagination or only exciting his emotions. You cannot tell even by reading the story for yourself. Its badness proves very little. The more imagination the reader has, being an untrained reader, the more he will do for himself. He will, at a mere hint from the author, flood wretched material with suggestion and never guess that he is himself chiefly making what he enjoys. The nearest we can come to a test is by asking whether he often *re-reads* the same story.

It is, of course, a good test for every reader of every kind of book. An unliterary man may be defined as one who reads books once only. There is hope for a man who has never read Malory or Boswell or *Tristram Shandy* or Shakespeare's *Sonnets*: but what can you do with a man who says he 'has read' them, meaning he has read them once, and thinks that this settles the matter? Yet I think the test has a special application to the matter in hand. For excitement, in the sense defined above, is just what must disappear from a second reading. You cannot, except at the first reading, be really curious about what happened. If you find that the reader of popular romance—however uneducated a reader, however bad the romances—goes back to his old favourites again and again, then you have pretty good evidence that they are to him a sort of poetry.

The re-reader is looking not for actual surprises (which can come only once) but for a certain ideal surprisingness. The

point has often been misunderstood. The man in Peacock
thought that he had disposed of 'surprise' as an element in
landscape gardening when he asked what happened if you
walked through the garden for the second time. Wiseacre! In
the only sense that matters the surprise works as well the
twentieth time as the first. It is the *quality* of unexpectedness,
not the *fact* that delights us. It is even better the second time.
Knowing that the 'surprise' is coming we can now fully relish
the fact that this path through the shrubbery doesn't *look* as if it
were suddenly going to bring us out on the edge of the cliff. So
in literature. We do not enjoy a story fully at the first reading.
Not till the curiosity, the sheer narrative lust, has been given
its sop and laid asleep, are we at leisure to savour the real
beauties. Till then, it is like wasting great wine on a ravenous
natural thirst which merely wants cold wetness. The children
understand this well when they ask for the same story over and
over again, and in the same words. They want to have again the
'surprise' of discovering that what seemed Little-Red-Riding-
Hood's grandmother is really the wolf. It is better when you
know it is coming: free from the shock of actual surprise you can
attend better to the intrinsic surprisingness of the *peripeteia*.

I should like to be able to believe that I am here in a very
small way contributing (for criticism does not always come
later than practice) to the encouragement of a better school of
prose story in England: of story that can mediate imaginative
life to the masses while not being contemptible to the few. But
perhaps this is not very likely. It must be admitted that the art
of Story as I see it is a very difficult one. What its central
difficulty is I have already hinted when I complained that in
the *War of the Worlds* the idea that really matters becomes lost
or blunted as the story gets under way. I must now add that
there is a perpetual danger of this happening in all stories. To
be stories at all they must be series of events: but it must be
understood that this series—the *plot*, as we call it—is only really
a net whereby to catch something else. The real theme may be,
and perhaps usually is, something that has no sequence in it,
something other than a process and much more like a state
or quality. Giantship, otherness, the desolation of space, are
examples that have crossed our path. The titles of some stories
illustrate the point very well. *The Well at the World's End*—can
a man write a story to that title? Can he find a series of events

following one another in time which will really catch and fix and bring home to us all that we grasp at on merely hearing the six words? Can a man write a story on Atlantis—or is it better to leave the word to work on its own? And I must confess that the net very seldom does succeed in catching the bird. Morris in the *Well at the World's End* came near to success—quite near enough to make the book worth many readings. Yet, after all, the best moments of it come in the first half.

But it does sometimes succeed. In the works of the late E. R. Eddison it succeeds completely. You may like or dislike his invented worlds (I myself like that of *The Worm Ouroboros* and strongly dislike that of *Mistress of Mistresses*) but there is here no quarrel between the theme and the articulation of the story. Every episode, every speech, helps to incarnate what the author is imagining. You could spare none of them. It takes the whole story to build up that strange blend of renaissance luxury and northern hardness. The secret here is largely the style, and especially the style of the dialogue. These proud, reckless, amorous people create themselves and the whole atmosphere of their world chiefly by talking. Mr. de la Mare also succeeds, partly by style and partly by never laying the cards on the table. Mr. David Lindsay, however, succeeds while writing a style which is at times (to be frank) abominable. He succeeds because his real theme is, like the plot, sequential, a thing in time, or quasi-time: a passionate spiritual journey. Charles Williams had the same advantage, but I do not mention his stories much here because they are hardly pure story in the sense we are now considering. They are, despite their free use of the supernatural, much closer to the novel; a believed religion, detailed character drawing, and even social satire all come in. *The Hobbit* escapes the danger of degenerating into mere plot and excitement by a very curious shift of tone. As the humour and homeliness of the early chapters, the sheer 'Hobbitry', dies away we pass insensibly into the world of epic. It is as if the battle of Toad Hall had become a serious *heimsókn* and Badger had begun to talk like Njal. Thus we lose one theme but find another. We kill—but not the same fox.

It may be asked why anyone should be encouraged to write a form in which the means are apparently so often at war with the end. But I am hardly suggesting that anyone who can write great poetry should write stories instead. I am rather suggesting what those whose work will in any case be a romance should aim at. And I do not think it unimportant that good work in this kind, even work less than perfectly good, can come where poetry will never come.

Shall I be thought whimsical if, in conclusion, I suggest that this internal tension in the heart of every story between the theme and the plot constitutes, after all, its chief resemblance to life? If story fails in that way does not life commit the same blunder? In real life, as in a story, something must happen. That is just the trouble. We grasp at a state and find only a succession of events in which the state is never quite embodied. The grand idea of finding Atlantis which stirs us in the first chapter of the adventure story is apt to be frittered away in mere excitement when the journey has once been begun. But so, in real life, the idea of adventure fades when the day-to-day details begin to happen. Nor is this merely because actual hardship and danger shoulder it aside. Other grand ideas—homecoming, reunion with a beloved—similarly elude our grasp. Suppose there is no disappointment; even so—well, you are here. But now, something must happen, and after that something else. All that happens may be delightful: but can any such series quite embody the sheer state of being which was what we wanted? If the author's plot is only a net, and usually an imperfect one, a net of time and event for catching what is not really a process at all, is life much more? I am not sure, on second thoughts, that the slow fading of the magic in *The Well at the World's End* is, after all, a blemish. It is an image of the truth. Art, indeed, may be expected to do what life cannot do: but so it has done. The bird has escaped us. But it was at least entangled in the net for several chapters. We saw it close and enjoyed the plumage. How many 'real lives' have nets that can do as much?

In life and art both, as it seems to me, we are always trying to catch in our net of successive moments something that is not successive. Whether in real life there is any doctor who can teach us how to do it, so that at last either the meshes will become fine enough to hold the bird, or we be so changed that we can throw our nets away and follow the bird to its own country, is not a question for this essay. But I think it is sometimes done—or very, very nearly done—in stories. I believe the effort to be well worth making.

POETIC DICTION AND LEGAL FICTION

OWEN BARFIELD

THE house of poetry contains many mansions. These mansions are so diverse in their qualities and in their effect on the indweller and some of them are so distant from others that the inhabitants of one mansion have sometimes been heard to deny that another is part of the same building at all. For instance, Edgar Allen Poe said that there is no such thing as a long poem, and the difference between a long narrative poem and a short lyric is admittedly rather baffling, seeming almost to be one of kind. What I have to say here touches mainly lyric poetry, and will interest those who love to dwell with recurring delight on special felicities of expression more than those to whom poetry means taking their *Iliad* or their *Faerie Queene* a thousand lines at a time and enjoying the story. It is highly specialized. Think for a moment of poems as of pieces of fabric, large tapestries, or minute embroideries as the case may be. What I have to say does not concern the whole form of even one of the embroideries, but only the texture itself, the nature of the process at any given point, as the fabric comes into being, the movements which the shuttle or the needle must have made. It is still more specialized than this; for in examining the texture of poetry one of the most important elements (a mansion to itself) is rhythm, sound, music; and all this is of necessity excluded. I am fully aware that this involves the corollary that the kind of poetry I am talking about may also be written in prose; but that is a difficulty which is chronic to the subject. I wish, however, to treat of that element in poetry which is best called 'meaning' pure and simple. Not the meaning of poetry, nor the meaning of any poem as a whole, but just meaning. If this sounds like an essay in microscopy, or if it be objected that what I am talking about is not poetic diction, but etymology or philosophy or even genetic psychology, I can only reply that whatever it ought to be called, it is, to some people, extraordinarily interesting, and that if, in all good faith, I have given it a wrong address, it is still to me the roomiest, the most commodious, and the most exciting of all the mansions which I rightly or wrongly include in the plan and elevation of the great house.

The language of poetry has always been in a high degree *figurative*; it is always illustrating or expressing what it wishes to put before us by comparing that with something else. Sometimes the comparison is open and avowed, as when Shelley compares the skylark to a poet, to a high-born maiden, and to a rose embowered in its own green leaves; when Keats tells us that a summer's day is:

> like the passage of an angel's tear
> That falls through the clear ether silently.

or when Burns writes simply: 'My love is like a red red rose.' And then we call it a 'simile'. Sometimes it is concealed in the form of a bare statement, as when Shelley says of the west wind, not that it is *like*, but that it *is* 'the breath of Autumn's being', calls upon it to 'make him its lyre' and says of himself that *his* leaves are falling. This is known as 'metaphor'. Sometimes the element of comparison drops still farther out of sight. Instead of saying that A is like B or that A is B, the poet simply talks about B, without making any overt reference to A at all. You know, however, that he intends A all the time, or, better say that you know he intends *an* A; for you may not have a very clear idea of what A is and even if you have got an idea, somebody else may have a different one. This is generally called 'symbolism'.

I do not say that these particular methods of expression are an absolute *sine qua non* of poetic diction. They are not. Poetry may also take the form of simple and literal statement. But figurative expression is found everywhere; its roots descend very deep, as we shall see, into the nature, not only of poetry, but of language itself. If you took away from the stream of European poetry every passage of a metaphorical nature, you would reduce it to a very thin trickle indeed, pure though the remainder beverage might be to the taste. Perhaps our English poetry would suffer the heaviest damage of all. Aristotle, when treating of diction in his *Poetics*, provides the right expression by calling the element of metaphor πολὺ μέγιστον—far the most important.

It may be noticed that I am now using the word 'metaphor' in a slightly different and wider sense than when I placed it in the midst between simile on the one hand and symbol on the other. I am now using it, and shall use it frequently throughout this article, to cover the whole gamut of figurative language including simile and symbol. I do not think this need confuse us. Strict metaphor occurs about the middle of the gamut and expresses the essential nature of such language more perfectly perhaps than either of the extremes. In something the same way Goethe found that the leaf of a plant expressed its essential nature as plant, while the blossom and the root could be considered as metamorphoses of the leaf. Here I want to try and consider a little more closely what the essential nature of figurative language is and how that nature is most clearly apparent in the figure called metaphor.

But first of all let us return to the 'gamut' and take some examples. This time let us move along it in the reverse direction, beginning from symbolism.

> Does the road wind uphill all the way?
> Yes, to the very end.
> Will the day's journey take the whole long day?
> From morn to night, my friend.
>
> But is there for the night a resting-place?
> A roof for when the slow, dark hours begin.
> May not the darkness hide it from my face?
> You cannot miss that inn.
>
> Shall I meet other wayfarers at night?
> Those who have gone before.
> Then must I knock or call when just in sight?
> They will not keep you waiting at that door.
>
> Shall I find comfort, travel-sore and weak?
> Of labour you shall find the sum.
> Will there be beds for me and all who seek?
> Yea, beds for all who come.

As I have already suggested, the ordinary way of characterizing this kind of language would be to say that the poet says one thing and means another. Is this true? Is it fair to say that Christina Rossetti says B but that she *really means* A? I do not think this is a question which can be answered with a simple 'yes' or 'no'. In fact the difficult and elusive relation between A and B is the heart of my matter. For the time being let me hazard, as a rather hedging sort of answer, that the truer it is to say 'yes', the worse is the poem, the truer it is to say 'no', the better is the poem. We feel that B, which is actually said, ought to be necessary, even inevitable in some way. It ought to be in some sense the best, if not the only way, of expressing A satisfactorily. The mind should dwell on it as well as on A and thus the two should be somehow inevitably fused together into one simple meaning. But if A is too obvious and could be equally or almost as well expressed by other and more direct means, then the mind jumps straight to A, remains focused on it, and loses interest in B, which shrinks to a kind of dry and hollow husk. I think this is a fault of Christina Rossetti's poem. We know just what A is. A = 'The good life is an effort' plus 'All men are mortal'. Consequently it detaches itself from B, like a soul leaving a body, and the road and the inn and the beds are not a real road and inn and beds, they look faintly heraldic—or as if portrayed in lacquer. They are not even poetically real. We never get a fair chance to accord to their existence that willing suspension of disbelief which we are told constitutes 'poetic faith'. Let us try another:

'Is there anybody there?' said the Traveller,
   Knocking on the moonlit door;
And his horse in the silence champed the grasses
   Of the forest's ferny floor:
And a bird flew up out of the turret,
   Above the Traveller's head:
And he smote upon the door again a second time:
   'Is there anybody there?' he said.
But no one descended to the Traveller;
   No head from the leaf-fringed sill
Leaned over and looked into his grey eyes,
   Where he stood perplexed and still.
But only a host of phantom listeners
   That dwelt in the lone house then
Stood listening in the quiet of the moonlight
   To that voice from the world of men:
Stood thronging the faint moonbeams on the dark stair,
   That goes down to the empty hall,
Hearkening in an air stirred and shaken
   By the lonely Traveller's call.
And he felt in his heart their strangeness,
   Their stillness answering his cry,
While his horse moved, cropping the dark turf,
   'Neath the starred and leafy sky;
For he suddenly smote on the door, even
   Louder, and lifted his head:—

'Tell them I came, and no one answered,
  That I kept my word', he said.
Never the least stir made the listeners,
  Though every word he spake
Fell echoing through the shadowiness of the still house
  From the one man left awake:
Ay, they heard his foot upon the stirrup
  And the sound of iron on stone,
And how the silence surged softly backward,
  When the plunging hoofs were gone.

This poem seems to me to possess as symbolism most of the
virtues which I miss in Christina Rossetti's. First it obviously
is a symbol. There *is* an A and a good solid one, though we
do not know what it is, because we cannot put it into a separate
container of words. But that is just the point. A has not got
(perhaps I should say, it has not *yet* got) a separate existence
in our apprehension; so it makes itself felt by modifying and
enriching the meaning of B—it hides itself in B, hides itself in
language which still *could* on the face of it be heard and inter-
preted as though no A came into the question at all.

I must here remark that merely making A obscure is not in
itself a recipe for writing good symbolical poetry. William Blake
at his worst, and, I fancy, many modern poets who write or
intend to write symbolically, go astray here. They are so
anxious to avoid the error of intending too obvious an A,
so anxious to avoid a mere old-fashioned simile, that we end by
being mystified or disgusted by the impossibility of getting any
sort of feeling at all of what they are talking about, or why. Why
are they talking about B at all, we ask ourselves. If they are
doing it simply for the sake of B, it is pure drivel. On the other
hand, if they intend an A, what evidence is there of it? We do
not mind A being intangible, because it is still only half born
from the poet's unconscious, but you cannot make poetry by
cunningly removing all the clues which, if left, would discover
the staleness of your meaning. In other words, if you set out to
say one thing and mean another, you must really mean another,
and that other must be worth meaning.

It will be observed that when we started from the simile and
moved towards the symbol, the criterion or yard-stick by which
we measured our progress was the element of *comparison*—para-
mount in the simile and very nearly vanished out of sight in the

symbol. When, on the other hand, we move backwards, starting from the symbol, we find ourselves with another yard-stick, viz. the fact of saying one thing and meaning another. The poet says B but he means A. He hides A in B. B is the normal every-day meaning which the words so to speak 'ought' to have on the face of them, and A is what the poet *really* has to say to us, and which he can only say through or alongside of, or by modifying, these normal everyday meanings. A is his own new, original, or poetic meaning. If I were writing this article in Greek or German, my public would no doubt be severely restricted, but there would be this advantage to me—that I could run the six words 'say-one-thing-and-mean-another' together and use the resulting conglomerate as a noun throughout the rest of it. I cannot do this, but I will make bold to borrow another German word instead. The word *Tarnung* was, I believe, extensively used under the heel of the Nazi tyranny in Germany for the precautionary practice of hiding one meaning in another, the allusion being to the *Tarnhelm* of the Nibelungs. I shall give it an English form and call it 'Tarning'. When I say 'Tarning', therefore, the reader is asked to substitute mentally the concept of saying one thing and meaning another, in the sense in which I have just been trying to expound it. We have already seen that the more A lives as a modification or enrichment of B, the better is the tarning.

Now let us proceed to the next step in our backward progress from symbol to simile. We come to the metaphor. And here we find both the best and the most numerous examples of tarn-ing. Almost any poem, almost any passage of really vivid prose which you pick up is sure to contain them in abundance. I will choose an example (the source of which he does not disclose) given by Dr. Hugh Blair, the eighteenth-century writer on style.

'Those persons who gain the hearts of most people, who are chosen as the companions of their softer hours, and their reliefs from anxiety and care, are seldom persons of shining qualities or strong virtues: it is rather *the soft green* of the soul on which we rest our eyes, that are fatigued with beholding more glaring objects.'

Consider how the ordinary literal meaning of the word 'green' blends with the ineffable psychic quality which it is the writer's object to convey! How much weaker it would be, had he written: 'It is rather persons whose souls we find restful, as the

eye finds green fields restful, &c.' Put it that way and nearly
all the tarning, and with it half the poetry, is lost. The passage
reminds me of this from Andrew Marvell's *Garden*:

> The Mind, that Ocean where each kind
> Does straight its own resemblance find;
> Yet it creates, transcending these,
> Far other Worlds, and other Seas;
> Annihilating all that's made
> To a green Thought in a green Shade.

What a lot of tarning can be done with the word 'green'!

We see that any striking and original use of even a single
word tends to be metaphorical and shows us the process of
tarning at work. On the whole, I think it is true to say that the
fewer the words containing the metaphor, the more the expression is in the strict sense a 'trope' rather than a metaphor—the
more tarning we shall feel. For the long and elaborate metaphor is already almost a simile—a simile with the word 'like'
missed out. We must, however, remember that the tarning
may not have actually occurred in the particular place where
we find it. People copy one another and the metaphor may be
a cliché or, if not a cliché, part of our common heritage of
speech. Thus, when Tennyson writes:

> When the happy Yes
> Falters from her lips,
> Pass and blush the news
> Over glowing ships

we feel that the peculiarly effective use of the word 'blush'
throughout this lyric is a tarning of his own. It actually goes on
in us as we read. When, on the other hand, Arnold writes in
the *Scholar Gypsy*:

> O Life unlike to ours!
> Who fluctuate idly without term or scope

or:
> Vague half-believers of our casual creeds,
> Who never deeply felt, nor clearly willed,
> Whose insight never has borne fruit in deeds

though none of this writing can be described as cliché, yet
we feel that the metaphorical element in 'fluctuate' and in
'borne fruit' is the product of a tarning that happened before
Arnold was born. So, too, in the passage I first quoted the

'*shining* qualities' and the '*softer* hours' are metaphors of the kind we are all using every day, almost without thinking of them as metaphors. We all speak of *clear* heads, of *brilliant* wit, of *seeing* somebody's meaning, of so and so being the *pick of the bunch*, and so on: and most of us must use at least, say, a hundred of these dead or half-dead metaphors every day of our lives. In fact, in dealing with metaphor, we soon find ourselves talking, not of poetry, but of language itself. Everywhere in language we seem to find that the process of tarning, or something very like it, either is or has been at work.

We seem to owe all these tropes and metaphors embedded in language to the fact that somebody at some time had the wit to say one thing and mean another, and that somebody else had the wit to tumble to the new meaning, to detect the bouquet of a new wine emanating from the old bottle. We owe them all to tarning, a process which we find prolifically at work wherever there is poetry—from the symbol, where it shouts at us and is all too easily mishandled, to the simile, where we already hear the first faint stirrings of its presence, inasmuch as the B image even here is modified, enriched, or coloured by the A image with which it is this time overtly compared.

> Then fly our greetings, fly our speech and smiles!
> —As some grave Tyrian trader, from the sea,
>   Descried at sunrise an emerging prow
> Lifting the cool-hair'd creepers stealthily,
>   The fringes of a southward-facing brow
>   Among the Aegean isles;
> And saw the merry Grecian coaster come,
>   Freighted with amber grapes, and Chian wine,
>   Green bursting figs, and tunnies steep'd in brine;
> And knew the intruders on his ancient home,
>
> The young light-hearted masters of the waves.

The grave Tyrian trader and the merry Grecian coaster are not the same figures that we should meet in a history book. They have their own life, they take in the imagination a special colour from the things with which they are compared—that is, the *Scholar Gypsy* on the one hand and our too modern selves on the other. They are pregnant with the whole of the poem that has gone before.

I said at the beginning that I might be accused of indulging in a kind of aesthetic microscopy. The drawback of the microscope is this, that even if the grain of sand which we see through it does indeed contain a world, mere magnification is not enough to enable us to see that world. Unfortunately the processes which are said to give to the infinitesimal a cosmic character are not merely minute; they are also very rapid. This is certainly true of the process of tarning as it takes place in the mind of the poet and his reader. It is both rapid and delicate and, as the reader may have felt already, it is difficult to take it out and examine it without rushing in where angels fear to tread. But there is another modern invention which may be brought to the aid of the microscope in order to meet this drawback; and that is the slow-motion film. Can we find in any sphere of human life something analogous to a slow-motion picture of the tarning process? I think we can. I have said that tarning can be detected not only in accredited poetry or literature but also in the history of language as a whole. Is there any other human institution in which tarning also happens, and in which it happens on a broader scale and at a more leisurely pace? I think there is. I think we shall find such an illustration as we want in the law, notably in the development of law by means of fictions.

We are accustomed to find something crabbed and something comic in legal fictions. When we read in an old pleading an averment that the plaintiff resides in the Island of Minorca, 'to wit in the parish of St. Mary le Bow in the Ward of Cheap' —or, in a Note in the *Annual Practice* for 1945, that every man-of-war is deemed to be situated permanently in the parish of Stepney—it sounds funny. But it must be admitted that it is not any funnier *per se* than Shelley's telling us that his leaves are falling or Campion informing us as to his mistress that 'there is a garden in her face'. It is funny when we take it literally, not particularly funny when we understand what is meant and why it is expressed in that particular way.

There is one kind of metaphor which occurs both in law and in poetry and which is on the whole commoner and less odd-sounding in modern law than it is in modern poetry. This is personification of abstractions:

> Let not Ambition mock their useful toil,
>   Their homely joys, and destiny obscure;
> Nor Grandeur hear with a disdainful smile
>   The short and simple annals of the poor.

We find this particular usage almost vanished from English poetry by the beginning of the twentieth century. The personification of abstractions and attributes which we find in the more high-flown sort of eighteenth-century poetry or in the occasional allegorical papers which Johnson inserted in the *Rambler* sound stiff and unnatural to us, and a modern poet would hardly bring himself to try and introduce the device at all. On the other hand, the personification of limited companies by which they are enabled to sue and be sued at law, to commit trespasses, and generally to be spoken of as carrying on all sorts of activities which can only *really* be carried on by sentient beings, is as common as dirt and no one ever dreams of laughing at it. But these examples will hardly do for our slow-motion picture. On the contrary, in them the gap between the B meaning and the A meaning is as wide and the prima facie absurdity of the B or surface-meaning is hardly less than in, let us say, Ossian's description of the Hero: 'In peace, thou art the Gale of Spring, in war, the Mountain Storm.'

The important thing is to see how and why the legal fiction comes into being and what is its positive function in the life of human beings. If you have suffered a wrong at the hands of another human being, the practical question for you, the point at which law really touches your life as a member of society, is, can you do anything about it? Can you bring the transgressor to book and obtain restitution? In other words, can you bring an action against him, obtain judgement, and get that judgement executed? Now the answer to that question must always depend to some extent, and in the earlier stages of a society governed by law it depends to a very large extent indeed on the answer to another question. It is not enough simply to show that the transgressor has, in common parlance, broken the law. What you or your advisers have to make up your mind about is something rather different and often much more complicated. You have to ask yourselves, Is there a form of procedure under which I can move against him? If so, is it sufficiently cheap and expeditious for me to be able to adopt it with some hope of success? Where, as in the case of English Common Law down to the middle of the nineteenth century, these forms of procedure, or forms of action as they are more often called, are severely restricted in number, these questions are very serious ones indeed.

While the so-called 'historical' fictions (which are the only ones I am concerned with) have no doubt played a broadly similar part in every known system of law, I think it will be best if I confine myself to England and take a particular example. The forms of action were not the arbitrary inventions of an ingenious legislator. They grew up out of the whole history of English social life, and one of the results of this was a wide difference between those forms of action which had their roots in the feudal system and those which sprang from later and different sources. I think it is true to say that they were different because they were really based on two different ways of looking at human beings in society. You may look at a human being in what I will call the genealogical way, in which case you will conceive of his legal rights and position as being determined by what he *is* rather than by what he may choose to *do*. They will then seem to be determined by the kind of father he had, by the piece of land to which he and his ancestors were attached or which was attached to them, and by its relations to adjoining land attached to other people and their ancestors and descendants. Or alternatively you may look at him in what I will call the personal way, in which case his position will seem to be determined more by the things which he himself has chosen to *do* of his own free will. Maine in his *Ancient Law* calls the first way 'Status' and the second way 'Contract', and he depicts society as evolving from the first towards the second. Broadly speaking, forms of action having to do with the ownership of land had grown up out of the first way, forms of action having to do with the ownership of personal property out of the second way, of looking at human beings.

Now suppose you had a good claim to the ownership of a piece of land, perhaps with a pleasant house on it, which was in the possession of somebody else who also, but wrongfully, claimed to be the owner. Your proper normal form of action, say, 500 years ago, was by Writ of Right, a form of action which was very much of the first type and hedged about accordingly with all sorts of ceremonies, difficulties, and delays.

At trahere atque moras tantis licet addere rebus!

One of the drawbacks of this type of action was that it was subject to things called *Essoins*. Essoins seem to have corresponded roughly to what we should call 'adjournments'; they no doubt grew up procedurally with a view to preventing an unscrupulous plaintiff from taking unfair advantage of the defendant's ill health, absence, or other accidental disability. But they must have been corn in Egypt for a usurping defendant. I am tempted to let Glanville,[1] in his own sedate language and at his own pace, give the reader some idea of their nature and complexity:

'If the Tenant, being summoned, appear not on the first day, but Essoin himself, such Essoin shall, if reasonable, be received; and he may, in this manner, essoin himself three times successively; and since the causes on account of which a person may justly essoin himself are various, let us consider the different kinds of Essoins.

'Of Essoins, some arise on account of ill health, others from other sources.'

(I will here interpose that, among the Essoins arising from other sources were the *de ultra mare* and the *de esse in peregrinatione* and that, if a person cast the Essoin *de esse in peregrinatione*, 'it must be distinguished whether he went to Jerusalem or to another place. If to the former place, then a year and a day at least is generally allowed him.' And with that I will let Glanville proceed again in his own order:)

'Of those Essoins which arise from ill health, one kind is that *ex infirmitate veniendi*, another *ex infirmitate de reseantisa*.

'If the Tenant, being summoned, should on the first day cast the Essoin *de infirmitate veniendi*, it is in the election of his Adversary, being present, either to require from the Essoiner a lawful proof of the truth of the Essoin in question on that very day, or that he should find pledges or bind himself solemnly that at the day appointed he will have his Warrantor of the Essoin . . . and he may thus Essoin himself three times successively. If on the third day, he neither appear nor essoin himself, then let it be ordered that he be forthcoming in person on another day; or that he send a fit Attorney in his place, to gain or lose for him. . . . It may be asked, what will be the consequence if the Tenant appear at the fourth day, after having cast three Essoins, and warrant all the Essoins? In that case, he shall prove the truth of each Essoin by his own oath and that of another; and, on the same day, he shall answer to the suit. . . .

'If anyone desire to cast the Essoin *de infirmitate de reseantisa*, he may thrice do it. Yet should the Essoiner, on the third day preceding that appointed, at a proper place and before a proper person,

---

[1] Beame's *Translation of Glanville*, London, 1812.

present his Essoin. If, on the third Summons the Tenant appear not, the Court should direct that it may be seen whether his indisposition amount to a languor, or not. For this purpose let the following Writ issue, directed to the Sheriff of the County . . .:

' "The King to the Sheriff, Health. I command you that, without delay, you send 4 lawful men of your County to see if the infirmity of which B. hath essoined himself in my Court, against R., be a languor or not. And, if they perceive that it is a languor, then, that they should put to him a day of one year and one day, from that day of the view, to appear before me or my justices. . . ." '

Nor was it forgotten that Essoiners themselves may be subject to infirmities and languors:

'The principal Essoiner is also at liberty, if so disposed, to essoin himself by another Essoiner. In this case the second Essoiner must state to the Court that the Tenant, having a just cause of Essoin, had been detained, so that he could not appear at the day appointed, neither to lose nor gain, and that therefore he had appointed a certain other person to essoin him; and that the Essoiner himself had met with such an impediment, which had prevented his appearance on that day: and this he is prepared to prove according to the practice of the Court. . . .'

Having at last succeeded in getting your opponent out of bed and fixing the day for the trial, you still could not be certain that he would not appear in Court followed (subject, no doubt, to Essoins) by a professional boxer or swordsman, whom you would have to tackle in lieu of calling evidence. And so on. And all this maybe about a claim so clear that you could get it disposed of in five minutes if you could only bring it to the stage of being tried at all!

It would have been a very different matter, so perhaps your Counsel would advise you, if only the issue were about *personal* property instead of real property. We could go to a different Court with a different form of action. No essoins. No wager of law. No trial by battle. No trial by ordeal. Everything up to date and efficient. What *is* personal property, you might ask. Well, your horse for one thing and your hawk and your clothes and your money—oh! yes, and oddly enough if you were a lease-holder instead of a freeholder and had only a term of years in this precious piece of land, *that* would be personal property too. But can't I get *my* case heard by these people? Don't they understand anything about fee simple? Oh! yes, they understand it all right; in fact they often have to decide the point. For instance, if a leaseholder in possession is ousted by a trespasser—by Jove! I've just thought of something! And then if your Counsel had a touch of creative genius, he might perhaps evolve the following device. It *was* evolved at all events, by Tudor times or thereabouts and continued in use down to the middle of the nineteenth century.

Remember the situation: You are the rightful owner of a piece of land of which X, who is in possession, wrongfully claims to be the owner. The device was this: you proceeded to inform the Court by your pleadings that you, as owner of the land, had recently leased it to a person whose name was John Doe, and John Doe had been ousted from his possession violently, *vi et armis*, by X, the Defendant. *You* were not bringing the action, you pretended: John Doe was; but as X might aver in his defence that the blameless Doe had no title, Doe has joined you, his landlord, in the proceedings to prove that you did have a good title at the time when you leased the land to him. By this means you got your case before the Court that had jurisdiction to deal with the action known as Ejectment, and were able to take advantage of the simpler and more effective procedure. Sometimes the fiction was a little more elaborate. Instead of alleging that X had ejected John Doe, you said that another gentleman called Richard Roe, or possibly William Stiles, had done so. Richard Roe having subsequently allowed X to take possession now claimed no interest in the proceedings, but he had given X notice that they were pending, so as to give X a chance to defend his title. In this case the first thing X heard of it all was a letter, signed 'your loving friend, Richard Roe', telling him what had happened. Needless to say, John Doe and Richard Roe had no existence.

Many thousands of actions of this pattern and using these names must have been brought between the fifteenth and the nineteenth centuries and before long the whole procedure was no doubt so much a matter of course that it was little more than a kind of mathematical formula. There must, however, have been some earlier occasions on which it was a good deal more, and it is upon any one of these—perhaps the first of all—that I want the reader to bend his mind. Picture to yourself the Court, with Counsel on his feet opening the case. The story of John Doe and Richard Roe is being unfolded. At one point the Judge suddenly looks up and looks very hard at Counsel, who either winks very slightly or returns a stolid uncomprehending stare according to his temperament and the intimacy of his acquaintance with the Judge out of hours. But Counsel knows all the same what has happened. The Bench has tumbled to it. The Judge has guessed that there is no John Doe, no Richard Roe, no lease, no entry, no ouster. At the same moment, however, the Judge has seen the point of the whole fiction, the great advantage in the speedy administration of justice (for the real issue—the validity of X's title and yours—will be heard fairly and in full) and in the extended jurisdiction of his own Court. He decides to accord to the pleadings that willing suspension of disbelief which hundreds of years later made Mr. Bumble say that the law was a 'hass'. The case proceeds. Place this picture before your mind's eye and there I think you will have a slow-motion picture of 'tarning'.

Has new law been made? It is much the same as asking whether new language has been made when a metaphor disappears into a 'meaning'. At all events, we begin to understand more fully what Maitland meant, when he wrote of English law that 'substantive law has at first the look of being gradually secreted in the interstices of procedure'. This is particularly true of an unwritten system like the English Common Law, where the law itself lay hidden in the unconscious, until it was expressed in a judgement, and where rights themselves depended on the existence of remedies. Consider that very important fiction, which is very much alive and flourishing all round us to-day—the fiction on which the law of trusteeship is based. Anyone who is a trustee will know how absurdly remote from reality is the B interpretation of his position, according to which he is the 'owner' of the trust property. Yet this fiction, which permeates the whole of our jurisprudence, which most certainly is law, and not merely procedure, was introduced in the first place by devices strictly procedural, devices and circumstances which had their origin in that same contrast between the genealogical and the personal conceptions of Society which gave us John Doe and Richard Roe.

Moreover, this fictitious ownership, which we call trusteeship, has been strong enough to have other fictions erected on it. By the Common Law the personal property of a married woman became her husband's as soon as she married. But by a particularly ingenious piece of tarning the equity judges expressed in the form of law, and in doing so no doubt partly created, a more modern view of the rights of married women. They followed the Common Law doctrine that the husband *owned* everything but, as to property which someone had given to the wife with the intention that she should have it for her own separate use, the Courts of Equity began in the eighteenth century to say that the husband did indeed own this, but he owned it as *trustee* for his wife; and they would prevent him from dealing with it in any other way.

In the same way a metaphor may be strong enough to support a metaphor, as when Shelley bids the west wind 'Make me thy lyre even as the forest is'. If Shelley is not a lyre, neither is the forest; yet he illustrates the one fiction with the other. Nor is there anything grotesque or strained in this magnificent line. It is only when we begin to ponder and analyse it that we see how daring it is.

The long analogy which I have been drawing may be expressed more briefly in the formula:— metaphor: language: meaning:: legal fiction : law : social life. It has no particular significance if poetry is to be regarded *only* as either a pleasurable way of diverting our leisure hours or a convenient vehicle for the propagation of doctrine. For it must be conceded that there is all the difference in the world between the propagation of a doctrine and the creation of a meaning. The doctrine is already formulated and, if we choose to express it by tarning, that is simply a matter of technique or political strategy. The creation of meaning is a very different matter. I hope I may have succeeded in showing in the earlier part of this article that metaphor is something more than a piece of the technique of one of the fine arts. It is πολὺ μέγιστον not merely in the diction of poetry but in the nature and growth of language itself. So far we have only considered in this connexion those ubiquitous figures of speech which are, or used to be, called 'tropes', as when we speak of our lives *fluctuating*, of our insight *bearing fruit* in deeds, of *seeing the point*, and so on. But if we proceed to study language with a more definitely historical bias, and look into the etymologies and derivations of words, then the vast majority even of those meanings which we normally regard as 'literal' are seen to have originated either in metaphors or in something like them. Such words as *spirit*, *sad*, *humour*, *perceive*, *attend, express, understand,* and so on immediately spring to the mind as examples. Indeed the difficulty here would rather be to find words that are *not* examples. There is no doubt that they were once metaphorical. The question which a good many people have asked themselves, a little uneasily, is, Are they *still* metaphors? And, if not, when—and still more *how*—precisely, did they cease to be so?

What is essential to the nature and growth of language is clearly essential to the nature and growth of our thought, or rather of our consciousness as a whole. In what way then is metaphor or tarning essential to that nature and that growth? Here we begin to tread on metaphysical ground and here I think the analogy of legal fictions can really help us by placing our feet on one or two firmer tufts in the quaking bog. It can help us to realize in firmer outlines certain concepts which, like all those relating to the nature of thought itself, are tenuous, elusive, and difficult of expression.

Students of history will have observed that rebellions and agitations arising out of dissatisfaction with the law tend, at any rate in the earlier stages of society, to demand, not so much a reform of the law as its *publication.* People complain that they do not know what the law is. They want to know what it is, because otherwise they cannot be sure that it will be the same to-morrow as it is to-day. In fact it is the very essence of a law that it should apply to every case. It follows that the forms of action must be limited in number, and they must not change from day to day. If there is a different law for every case that arises, then what is being administered is simply not law at all but the arbitrary (though not necessarily unjust) decisions of those who govern us. But that is exactly what the word law *means*—something which is *not* such a series of arbitrary decisions or events, something which will be *the same* for the next case as it was for the last. This is where the difficulty arises; for it is the nature of life itself (certainly of human life) never to repeat itself exactly. Phenomena exactly repeated are not life, they are mechanism. Life varies, law is of its nature unvarying. Yet at the same time it is the function of law to serve, to express, and indeed partly to *make* the social life of the community. That is the paradox, the diurnal solution of which constitutes the process called society. One solution is legislation, the other is fiction. Legislation is drastic, *a priori*, and necessary. Fiction is flexible, empirical, and also necessary. 'Without the Fiction of Adoption', says Maine in his *Ancient Law*, 'it is difficult to understand how Society would ever have escaped from its swaddling-clothes.'

In the paradoxical relation of law to social life I think we have a useful picture of the paradoxical relation of language to consciousness. Formal logic is not much studied nowadays, but that does not alter the fact that logic is essential to the very existence of language and the forms of proposition and syllogism underlie all expression. Now logic presupposes first and foremost that the same word means the same thing in one sentence as it does in another. Humpty Dumpty may speak of making his words 'mean' what he chooses, and if somebody made a noise never heard before or since he might possibly manage to convey some sort of vague sympathetic impression of the state of his feelings. Yet repetition is inherent in the very meaning of the word 'meaning'. To say a word 'means' something implies that it means that same something more than once.

Here then is the paradox again. The logical use of language presupposes the meanings of the words it employs and presupposes them constant. I think it will be found to be a corollary of this, that the logical use of language can never add any meaning to it. The conclusion of a syllogism is implicit already in the premises, that is, in the *meanings* of the *words* employed; and all the syllogism can do is to make that meaning clearer to us and remove any misconception or confusion. But life is not constant. Every man, certainly every original man, has something new to say, something new to mean. Yet if he wants to express that meaning (and it may be that it is only when he tries to express it, that he knows what he means) he must use language—a vehicle which presupposes that he must either mean what was meant before or talk nonsense!

If therefore he would say anything really new, if that which was hitherto unconscious is to become conscious, he must resort to tarning. He must talk what is nonsense on the face of it, but in such a way that the recipient may have the new meaning suggested to him. This is the true importance of metaphor. I imagine this is why Aristotle, in calling metaphor 'the most important', gives as a reason that 'it alone does not mean borrowing from someone else'. In terms of mixed law and logic we might perhaps say that the metaphorical proposition contains a judgement, but a judgement pronounced with a wink at the Court. Bacon put it more clearly in the *Advancement of Learning* when he said:

'Those whose conceits are seated in popular opinions need only but to prove or dispute; but those whose conceits are beyond popular opinions have a double labour; the one *to make themselves conceived*, and the other to prove and demonstrate. So that it is of necessity with them to have recourse to similitudes and translations to express themselves.'

If we consider Bacon's position in the history of thought, it will not surprise us that the problem should have presented itself to him so clearly. Himself a lawyer, was he not attempting to do for science the very thing which Maitland tells us those old legal fictions were contrived for, that is, 'to get modern results out of medieval premisses'?

At all events there is a sentence in the *Novum Organum* which provides one of the most striking illustrations of tarning that it would be possible to imagine. It is a double illustration: first, there was an attempt at deliberate and fully conscious meaning-making, which failed: Bacon tried to inject new meaning into a word by *saying* precisely what he wanted it to mean. But we have seen that what is said precisely cannot convey new meaning. But, since his meaning *was* really new, there had at some point in the process to be a piece of actual tarning. There was— and it succeeded. He did in fact inject new meaning into another word—not by saying, but by just meaning it!

'Licet enim in natura nihil vere existat praeter corpora individua edentia actus puros individuos ex lege; in doctrinis tamen, illa ipsa lex, ejusque inquisitio et inventio atque explicatio, pro fundamento est tam ad sciendum quam ad operandum. Eam autem legem ejusque paragraphos *formarum* nomine intelligimus; praesertim cum hoc vocabulum invaluerit, et familiariter occurrat.'[1]

The 'forms' of which Bacon here speaks were none other than the Platonic ideas, in which Bacon, of course, did not believe. What he did believe in was that system of abstract causes or uniformity which we have long since been accustomed to

---

[1] Although it is true that in nature nothing exists beyond separate bodies producing separate motions according to law; still for the *study* of nature that very law and its investigation discovery and exposition are the essential thing, for the purpose both of science and of practice. Now it is that law and its clauses which we understand by the term 'forms'—principally because this word is a familiar one and has become generally accepted. *Novum Organum*, ii. 2.

express by the phrase 'the laws of nature', but for which there was then no name, because the meaning was a new one. He therefore tried deliberately by way of a *simile* to put this new meaning into the old word '*forma*'; but he failed, inasmuch as the new meaning never came into general use. Yet at the same time, more unconsciously, and by way of *metaphor*, he was putting the new meaning into the word '*lex*' itself—that curious meaning which it now bears in the expression 'the laws of nature'. This is one of those pregnant metaphors which pass into the language, so that much of our subsequent thinking is based on them. To realize that after all they *are* metaphors, and to ask what that entails, opens up avenues of inquiry which are beyond the province of this article. Certainly, they may be misleading, as well as illuminating. Long after Bacon's time, two great men—a lawyer who was concerned with the nature of law and a poet who was concerned with the nature of Nature—felt bound to draw attention to this very metaphor.

'When an atheist', wrote Austin,[1] 'speaks of *laws* governing the irrational world, the metaphorical application is suggested by an analogy still more slender and remote. . . . He means that the uniformity of succession and co-existence resembles the uniformity of conduct produced by an imperative rule. If, to draw the analogy closer, he ascribes these laws to an author, he personifies a verbal abstraction and makes it play the legislator. He attributes the uniformity of succession and co-existence to *laws* set by *nature*: meaning by nature, the world itself; or perhaps that very uniformity which he imputes to nature's commands.'

The introduction of the atheist into this passage does not, I think, weaken its force as an illustration, for whatever the strength of Bacon's religious faith, it is quite plain that the 'laws' of which he speaks in the *Novum Organum* have very little to do with the 'commands' of any being other than nature itself.

'Long indeed', says Coleridge in *The Friend*, 'will man strive to satisfy the inward querist with the phrase, laws of nature. But though the individual may rest content with the seeming metaphor, the race cannot. If a law of nature be a mere generalization, it is included . . . as an act of the mind. But if it be other and more, and yet manifestable only in and to an intelligent spirit, it must in act and substance be itself spiritual; for things utterly heterogeneous can have no intercommunion.'

[1] *Jurisprudence* (1869), i. 213.

Perhaps we may supplement the last sentence by saying that an *apparent* intercommunion between things utterly heterogeneous is the true mark of metaphor and may be significant of spiritual substance. If this is so, and if the aptness of a metaphor to mislead varies inversely with the extent to which it continues to be felt and understood *as* a metaphor and is not taken in a confused way semi-literally, then the contemplation by the mind of legal fictions may really be a rather useful exercise. For these are devices of expression, of which the practical expediency can easily be understood, and whose metaphorical nature is not so easily forgotten as they pass into general use.

There is not much that is more important for human beings than their relations with each other, and it is these which laws are designed to express. The making and application of law are thus fundamental human activities, but what is more important for my purpose is that they.bear the same relation to naked thinking as travelling does to map-reading or practice to theory. It is not by accident that such key-words as *judgement* and *cause* have two distinct meanings; the practical task of fixing personal responsibility must surely have been the soil from which, as the centuries passed, the abstract notion of cause and effect was laboriously raised. Accordingly it would be strange indeed if the study of jurisprudence were not well adapted to throw light on the mind and its workings.

That study was formerly regarded as an essential element in a liberal education. It was a distinguished Italian jurist, Giovanni Battista Vico, who at the turn of the seventeenth and eighteenth centuries became interested in the figurative element in language and evolved therefrom a theory of the evolution of human consciousness from an instinctive 'poetic' wisdom (*sapienza poetica*) to the modern mode of analytical thought.

It is perhaps a pity that this respectful attitude to legal studies has long since been abandoned; a pity both on general grounds and because the vast change in man's idea of himself wrought by the new notions of evolution and development, and by the comparatively recent birth of historical imagination, have opened up rich new fields of speculation both in language and in law. A better and more widely diffused knowledge of the latter could hardly fail to be beneficial in far-reaching ways at a time when the whole theory of human society is in the melting-pot. For instance, a deeper, more sympathetic understanding of the long, slow movement of the human mind from the feudal, or genealogical, way of regarding human relationships towards what I have called the 'personal' way would do no harm.

But I have been mainly concerned here with the subject of fictions. Properly understood, are they not a telling illustration of the fact that knowledge—the fullest possible awareness—of the nature of law is the true way of escape from its shackles? ἐγὼ γὰρ διὰ νόμου νόμῳ ἀπέθανον, 'I, by the law, died unto the law', wrote St. Paul; and the *nature* of law, as law, is the same, whether it be moral, or logical, or municipal. If it be important for men to get a deep feeling for this process of liberation in general, it is equally important, for special reasons, that they should better comprehend the particular problem of the part played by metaphor in the operation and development of language. Here too the way to achieve liberation from the 'confusion' of thought on which metaphor is based is not by attack or rebellion. The intrinsic nature of language makes all such attitudes puerile. It is not those who, like the optimistic Mr. Stuart Chase,[1] set out to cut away and expose all metaphorical usage who escape the curse of Babel. No. The best way to talk clearly and precisely and to talk sense is to understand as fully as possible the relation between predication and suggestion, between 'saying' and 'meaning'. For then you will at least know what you are *trying* to do. It is not the freemen of a city who are likeliest to lose their way, and themselves, in its labyrinth of old and mazy streets; it is the simple-minded foreign nihilist making, with his honest-to-god intentions and suitcase, straight for the centre, like a sensible man.

[1] *The Tyranny of Words*, London, 1938.

NOTE.—The author expresses his thanks to Mr. de la Mare and to Messrs. Faber & Faber for permission to quote *The Listeners*.

MARRIAGE AND *AMOUR COURTOIS* IN LATE FOURTEENTH-CENTURY ENGLAND

GERVASE MATHEW

ANY attempt to analyse the relationship in late fourteenth-century England between the ideal of marriage and that of courtly love must begin with a recognition of the changing social structure of that time. For *l'amour courtois* was in its origins avowedly a class ideal, theoretically unattainable either by the vilain or the bourgeois: nor is there any evidence for its existence outside the limited, if fluid, knightly class and those who would wish to adopt its fashion.

At this period very little can be known of the unpropertied and the unprivileged, the peasants and farm servants in the country-side, the poorer artisans there or in the towns. We still possess some catchwords of the Peasants' Rising and a few rude paintings in some village churches; to them might be added the fragments of the ale-house songs in Rawlinson MS. D 913. But that is all. It may be possible to pierce through folk-song and folk custom to a medieval substratum and to find vestiges that suggest the late survival of much pre-Christian usage, notably in fertility cults; still the result would be inevitably hypothetic and only fitfully revealing. In late fourteenth-century England, 'as far as literary evidence can be assessed, the great mass of the people remain inarticulate.

But already there was a grouping throughout England that might be described as a middle class though its exact limits are difficult to determine. It might be said to include all those who possessed some property or some pride of status but who neither used nor aspired to use coat armour. For economic reasons it seems hardly to have been differentiated by the blurred distinction between town and country, except possibly in the north. To it would belong the guildsman in the town, many property-holders in the country, the reeve, the bailiff, the shipman, and the miller. This was a grouping that found its closest parallel in fourteenth-century Europe among the burgher class of the Hansa towns and Flanders. Partly this may have been the result of trade contacts and of the sustained predominance of East Anglia; the life of Margerie Kempe suggests how naturally

King's Lynn was orientated to Lübeck, Dantzig, and Cologne. Primarily it was due to the presence of similar factors in a similar setting, the slow growth of a trading community consciously divorced from the ideals of a would-be international knightly class. It is suggestive that when the romance *Octovian*[1] was recast for a new audience in south-east England about 1350, the *courtois* elements, most of the love matter, and the introspection were replaced by a new emphasis on the shrewd triumphs of the butcher Clement and on the hero's skill in wrestling and in throwing the weight. Difficult as it is to ascribe its exact public to any medieval text it still seems possible to reconstruct some of the current ideals of this class from the great mass of literary evidence that remains.

In late fourteenth-century England medieval religion seems at its strongest within this grouping which provided not only the great preachers (and perhaps much of their audiences) but also the religious vitality of the Lollard movement. Margerie Kempe and the tailor Badsby were both born in this milieu. But it is curious how much of its didactic literature and of the popular gnomic wisdom turns avowedly upon a profit motive. Strong in the emphasis upon objective right and wrong it yet suggests a world very remote from that of Froissart's public. The ideal of marriage is neither cynical nor ignoble but completely un-*courtois*. The little treatise in Balliol MS. 354 'How the gode man taught hys sone' is late fourteenth century in its present form. The wise father tells his son to marry for love, to cherish his wife, and never to strike or curse her, to rule her gently, and to remember that though his servant she is also in some sense his companion. In the parallel piece preserved in Ashmole MS. 61 f7 the 'gode Wyfe' instructs her daughter in what is in effect the *Hausfrau* ideal; a similar impression is conveyed by the Wycliffite tract 'of weddid men and wifes'[2] and in the verses on a girl's upbringing in the 'good Wyfe wold a Pylgremage'.[3] It is an ideal quite compatible with the crude humours of the York guild-plays; the conception of the wife as a household shrew has always been the obverse to the ideal of the wife as a *Hausfrau*. It should be noted that though love is seen as a natural concomitant and perhaps as the cause of marriage it is not love conceived in any *courtois* or even romantic sense;

---

[1] Ed. Weber, *Metrical Romances*, vol. iii, pp. 157 et seqq.
[2] Ed. Arnold, vol. iii, pp. 188 et seqq.   [3] Ed. E.E.T.S., E.S. (B).

the love of man for woman referred to in Balliol MS. 354 is to be based on character, not looks.

Perhaps the attitude of all this grouping to the courtly love of the knightly romances is best conveyed by four fourteenth-century lines:

> Love is a selkud wodeness
> That the idel man ledeth by wildernesse
> That thurstes of wilfulnesse.
> and drinket sorweness.[1]

A 'selkud wodeness', a madness, an *insania mentis*.

Apart from an economic interpretation of history it would be difficult to discern any adequate reason for the patent difference in ideals between the trading and the knightly class in the reign of Richard II. It is improbable that at this period there was any race-distinction between them though it seems clear that some such distinction was believed in.[2] The knightly class can have been only a very small minority;[3] its cadre was formed by the new court, the magnates with the gentlemen of their households; the small groups[4] of knightly families in each shire who now controlled so much of the machinery of local administration; and the group of knightly families within Wales who raised the dues and levies for their absent lords. This is a cross-section adequately represented by the witnesses in the case of Scrope *v.* Grosvenor. Consciously it was a small minority linked together by the use of heraldry at a time when this was still restricted even among the larger land-owners; it was welded by the acceptance of French knightly custom and in the case of many of its members by similar training in some great lord's household or by some experience of the wars. But an attempt to estimate the significance of its ideal of marriage for fourteenth-century England must take into account the fact that it possessed the prestige of fashion at a period when it was a commonplace of satirists that the soap-maker's son would wish to be knighted and the Franklin wished his son to be like the knight's. Sociologically it was long possible in England to combine the

[1] Ed. P. Meyer (Rom. iv, p. 382).

[2] Cf. the evidence of Sir Robert Latom in the case of Scrope *v.* Grosvenor (ed. 1879, vol. i, p. 111). (Cf. ed. Nicholas, vol. i, p. 301.)

[3] For the beginning of this period cf. N. Denholm Young, 'Feudal Society in the Thirteenth Century', *History*, September 1944.

[4] For the composition and political significance of this section cf. K. B. McFarlane, 'Parliament and Bastard Feudalism', *R. Hist. S. Transactions*, 1944, pp. 53 et seqq.

existence of clearly marked class distinctions with the fact that the classes flowed almost imperceptibly into one another. In the late fourteenth century, however great the value placed upon the possession of good blood, social status was in fact determined rather by training and by employment than by descent; Chaucer was to be unique as a poet, but in his official career he is a type. It was a society in which personal relationships held primary importance and in which the emotional content was provided by a romantic and perhaps adolescent conception of personal loyalty, friendship, and adventure.

At least within this milieu a conventional theory of marriage assumed that it was not only compatible with romantic love but ideally an expression of it. Owing to the conscious acceptance of French fashion such love was phrased in terms of that *amour courtois* first clearly formulated in twelfth-century France.

The place of *amour courtois* in medieval theory lies among the applications of the treatises *De Amicitia*. However deeply Ovid influenced its literary expression, its roots are with Cicero and Aristotle. Ultimately it seems based on the Ciceronian conception of friendship; the love of another for the other's sake. Because it is the love of another for the other's sake it finds its expression in giving and serving, not in getting, and is frustrated not when it fails to get but when it ceases to give. Therefore love service is the essential expression of *amour courtois*. In contrast to a blind and transient passion, *amour fol*, courtly love was conceived as *amour voulu*, an unchanging disposition of the individual will. It was the expression of an instinctive connaturality between two individuals and therefore could be conceived as part of the lover's nature. It was this that could provide a speculative basis for the emphasis on the vivid increase in all forms of sensibility which was held to follow from an experience that had affected the nature of the lover and for the emphasis on constancy as the test not so much of the sincerity as of the genuineness of a love. The 'turtel' in Chaucer's *Parlement of Foules* reflects this cult of an unchanging loyalty:

'Nay, God forbede a lover shulde chaunge!'
The turtel seyde, and wex for shame al reed;
'Thogh that his lady evermore be straunge,
Yet let him serve hir ever, til he be deed.'[1]

[1] The *Parlement of Foules*, ll. 582-5.

It is the same as the lesson that was first taught Troilus:

> Nay, nay, but ever in oon be fresh and grene
> To serve and love his dere hertes queene,
> And thenk it is a guerdon hir to serve
> A thousandfold more than he can deserve.[1]

And as the refrain of the fifth of John Gower's *Cinkante Balades* 'Pour tout le mond jeo ne la changeroie'.[2]

A fourteenth-century Anglo-Norman allegory preserved in the Arundel MSS. treats of the relationship between such love and marriage.[3] The imagery is influenced both by the *Romaunt of the Rose* and by Ovid. Love is a naked boy, yellow-haired and blind. He holds a dart and roses fly from him like sparks. His castle is raised on Loyalty and its keep is a loyal heart. His three enemies are Mistrust and Treason and their father False-hood, while Jealousy is the mangonel with which they attempt to breach his castle wall. He who loves worthily must be loyal and have a loyal heart. He must have courtesy and always speak courteously. He must honour all women and always speak well of them. He must be able to keep his own counsel and to keep chaste and to keep his mind from *lecherie et ordure*, and if his love is answered he will know himself to be unworthy and will do all things to increase the pleasure and honour of her who has answered it. They will take each other in holy church. But being married they remain *amys et amye* and such good loving rightly used can please and serve God and bring them to a joy without end.

A similar union of a romantic love and marriage is assumed in the majority of the knightly romances that took their present form in late fourteenth-century England. Love is at first sight, there is much emphasis on the increase in the hero's prowess and in his emotional sensibility, on his love symptoms and elaborate courtesies; the love service and the love obedience come from him. The love of *Sir Degrevaunt*[4] and Melydor analysed in detail in the northern dialect remains conventional *amour courtois*. But at the end Degrevaunt and Melydor live married for thirty years and have seven children.[5] *Sir Torrent*

---

[1] *Troilus and Criseyde*, ll. 816–19.
[2] Ed. G. C. Macaulay, *French Works of John Gower*, p. 342.
[3] Arundel MS. 14 (College of Arms). For the analysis of this allegory I am indebted to C. West, *Courtoisie in Anglo-Norman Literature*, pp. 144–50.
[4] Ed. in Camden Society 30, pp. 177–256; cf. ll. 513–76.
[5] Op. cit., ll. 1889–92.

of Portyngale[1] at last marries Desonel, *Sir Eglamour* Cristabelle,[2] *Sir Triamour*[3] the daughter of the King of Hungary; by 1400 the story of *Sir Otuel* has been altered[4] so that he can marry Belyssant.[5] A generation later the elaborate marriage plots in *Generydes*[6] illustrate how much the union of love and marriage has come to be assumed.

Again, probably as early as 1350, the romance of *William of Palerne*[7] took its present English form in the household of the Earl of Hereford.[8] It is essentially a *roman courtois*, with its conventional hero and well-lettered *courtoise* heroines. The love symptoms of William[9] and Melior[10] are those uniformly characteristic in French *courtoise* literature. Melior and William marry[11] and have sons. The elaborate composite romance of Partonope of Blois[12] may perhaps be dated soon after 1400. The plot centres on Partonope's disobedience to Melior and his eventual pardon:

> for in longe service it may happe that she
> wolde shew hyme of her benignyte.

Almost inevitably 'knytte in wedloke to gedre thei be'.[13] Between 1350 and 1400 there were three English redactions[14] of the Anglo-Norman love story of Ippomadon and La Fiere; La Fiere is again the typical heroine of a *roman courtois*, fair-haired, clear-eyed, self-controlled; Ippomadon makes himself her cup bearer and after the tournaments vows himself to be her servant always. They marry and have sons and after marriage are still described as lovers. The *Knightes Tale* expresses perfectly what had become the conventional and expected happy ending:

> and thus with alle blisse and melodye
> Hath Palamon y-wedded Emelye . . .
> And Emelye him loveth so tendrely
> And he hir serveth al so gentilly.[15]

'And he hir serveth al so gentilly.' For the conception of

[1] Ed. E.E.T.S., E.S. 51.
[2] Ed. Camden Society 30; for the marriage, l. 1297 et seq.; cf. ll. 145–80.
[3] Ed. Halliwell. Percy Society.
[4] In 'Duke Rowlande and Sir Ottuel', ed. E.E.T.S., E.S. 35 (p. 53 et seq.).
[5] Op. cit., l. 1583 et seq.   [6] E.E.T.S., 55.
[7] E.E.T.S., E.S. (1).   [8] l. 5529 et seq.
[9] Op. cit., ll. 732–87 and. 874–944.   [10] Op. cit., ll. 433–579.
[11] Op. cit., ll. 4832–5516.   [12] Ed. Bödtker (E.E.T.S., E.S. 109).
[13] Op. cit., l. 12152; cf. ll. 1220–60, 1824; ll. 5212–56; l. 10303 et seq.
[14] Ed. Kölbing.   [15] *Knightes Tale*, ll. 2239–40, 2245–46.

a constant love finding its expression in an unchanging love service logically alters the ideal of marriage from that of the husband's calm rule in the *Wyse Mans Advyse* into one of mutual service, mutual obedience:

> When Maistrie comth the God of love anon
> Beteth hise winges, and farewel, he is gon![1]

It finds its most explicit formulation in the *Frankeleyn's Tale*:[2]

> Thus hath she take hir servant and hir lord
> Servant in love and lord in marriage;
> Than was he bothe in lordship and servage;
> Servage? Nay, but in lordshipe above,
> Sith he hath bothe his lady and his love;
> His lady, certes, and his wyf also
> The which that lawe of love acordeth to.[3]

This is a conception paralleled more prosaically by John Gower in his use of the symbol of a Single Heart in the *Traitié selonc les auctours pour essampler les Amantz Marietz*.[4]

> Tout un soul coer eiont par tiel devis
> Loiale amie avoec loials amis.[5]

It is suggestive that those of Gower's *Cinkante Balades* which deal explicitly with marriage are phrased according to *amour courtois* in its contemporary Paris mode:[6]

> Tenetz ma foi, tenetz mes serementz;
> Mon coer remaint toutditz en vostre grace.[7]

Although there is in contrast the massed literature of disillusionment and of irony, this also is perhaps a witness to the prevalence of the ideals from which it was the reaction.

There can never be sufficient evidence to determine the exact extent to which the ideal of love and marriage in the romances either influenced or reflected contemporary social custom. Though child betrothals and family alliances were clearly common enough in the knightly class neither were necessarily

---

[1] *Frankeleyn's Tale*, ll. 37–8.
[2] Cf. Arviragus's resolution when he marries Dorigen to:
> 'hir obeye, and folwe hir wil in al
> As any lovere to his lady shal.'
> Ibid., ll. 21–2.
[3] Ibid. ll. 64–70.
[4] Ed. G. C. Macaulay, *French Works of John Gower*, pp. 379–92.
[5] Ibid., p. 381. [6] Ibid., pp. 338–42.
[7] *Cinkante Balades*, I. 4. ll. 3–4.

unaffected by it. It is significant that Richard II could conceive his marriage with Anne of Luxemburg in terms of a high-wrought and fantastic love, while the *Book of the Duchesse* shows that it was possible, and in fact fashionable, to describe the first marriage of John of Gaunt in phrases of pure *amour courtois*:

> In alle my youthe, in alle chaunce,
> She took me in hir governaunce.[1]

At least those who listened through the long-drawn chivalrous romances can never have forgotten the existence of an ideal of the relation between love and marriage. For it was a lesson almost monotonously inculcated by the barely individualized heroes and heroines as they flitted through plots formed by the tension of conflicting loyalties and surcharged with the fantastic adventures and the severances that are the tests of constancy.

[1] *Book of the Duchesse*, ll. 1285-6.

THE GALLEYS OF FRANCE

W. H. LEWIS

UNTIL the coming of the concentration camp, the galley held an undisputed pre-eminence as the darkest blot on Western civilization; a galley, said a poetic observer shudderingly, would cast a shadow in the blackest midnight. In the seventeenth century, the great age of the galleys, the particularly bad reputation of those of Louis XIV is fortuitous; all the Mediterranean powers possessed galleys, and the brutalities practised on those of other powers were often more horrible than anything that would have been tolerated in the French service. And the galleys can enter a strong plea in condonation of their existence, namely, that the convict existed for the galley, not the galley for the convict. The navies of the seventeenth century had to conform to the limited strategic and tactical plan imposed upon them by their two possible propellants, wind and oar; and in consequence the galley, with its perpetual mobility, was the important fast tactical unit of a Mediterranean navy. Until the coming of steam the galley, under many conditions of weather, was the fastest thing afloat on the inland sea; it composed to a considerable extent the scouting division of the fleet. In light airs the galleys, and only the galleys, could protect the coast against the Barbary pirate or hunt him down in the open sea; in a fleet action the galley was the only thing which could remove a damaged capital ship from its place in the line of battle; in amphibious operations its shallow draft made it the ideal landing-craft, whilst its main armament could engage closer inshore than that of the lightest vessels of the fleet proper. The galley was in fact indispensable.

The experiment of propelling galleys by free men hired for the oar had been tried and had failed; the commanders concerned had reported that with such a bank neither the speed nor the endurance essential could be obtained. Only the whip, with the threat of worse brutalities in reserve, could send the long, lean, cranky craft into action at the requisite speed. Given the necessity for the galley on the one hand, and a country swarming with criminals on the other, the *galérien* was the obvious, indeed the only, solution, the cheap fuel so callously expended in driving these fast ships.

Who was the typical *galérien*? The society of the bench fell into five distinct classes: Turks, bought by the French Government for the service, deserters, salt smugglers, genuine criminals, and, after 1685, Huguenots, the first category being definitely the least badly treated, and the last on the whole the worst. Even before the coming of the Huguenot, the *galériens* were by no means, as is often supposed, drawn exclusively from the dregs of France; at the battle of Genoa in 1638 the galley *La Cardinale* was saved by the exertions of a convict, the Chevalier de Margaillet, who was doing time for the rape of his niece; when Mlle de Scudéry was at Marseilles in 1644 she noticed that *galériens* of good social standing were allowed a considerable degree of liberty, and in their spare hours were to be met in the best *salons* of the town; in 1670 Mme de Sévigné is assured by the General of the Galleys that her protégé Valcroissant, a *galérien*, is 'living as he pleases, ashore in Marseilles, and without chains'. The conductor of the orchestra of the galley *La Palme* had been a performer in the private band of Louis XIV, had thrown up his post in a fit of pique, enlisted, and then deserted. And there were many other similar cases. In the earlier part of the reign the *galérien* is dumb, we catch a glimpse of him only from the outside, or at best we look down from the poop on his crowded misery.

'We went to visit the galleys,' writes Evelyn in 1644. 'The Captaine of the Galley Royal gave us a most courteous entertainment in his Cabine, the slaves in the interim playing both loud and soft musiq very rarely. Then he show'd us how he commanded their motions with a nod and his whistle, making them row out. The spectacle was to me new and strange, to see so many hundreds of miserably naked persons, having their heads shaven close and having only high red bonnets and payre of coarse canvas drawers, their whole backs and leggs naked and made fast to their seats about their middles and leggs in couples, and all commanded in a trice by an imperious and cruell seaman.... I was amaz'd to contemplate how these miserable catyfs lie in their galley crouded together, yet there is hardly one but had some occupation by which, as leisure and calms permitted, they gat some little money. Their rising and falling back at their oare is a miserable spectacle, and the noise of their chaines with the roaring of the beaten waters has something of strange and fearefull to one unaccustomed to it. They are rul'd and chastiz'd by strokes on their backs and soles of their feete on the least disorder and without the least humanity; yet they are cherefull and full of knavery.'

With the Revocation of the Edict of Nantes in 1685 the bench
becomes vocal, a light shines into the sinister interior of the
galley. From letters of Huguenot convicts, and the memoirs of
such as survived to write them after their release in 1712, we are
able to piece together a tolerably accurate account of the *galérien's*
life. Bad though the story is, it is not wholly bad; its sombre
texture is shot through with gleams of humanity, almost of
kindliness, for the officers were often less brutal than the system
which they administered.

Once condemned to the galleys, the convict was consigned
to the nearest jail where he might spend a considerable time in
almost any variety and degree of comfort or suffering whilst
awaiting the order for his transfer to the chain assembly-point—
Lille for the galleys of Dunkirk, Paris for those of Marseilles.
Their hands bound, and with an escort of provost's archers, the
sad little groups tramped the country roads which converged
on their last land prison. A Huguenot merchant, who was
condemned in 1701 for trying to escape from France, has left
us a description of the chain assembly-prison at Lille—a large
room in St. Peter's tower, so dark that day was but darkness
made visible, without fire or candle, a little broken straw,
innumerable rats and mice, and the society of thirty of the most
depraved scoundrels in France. . . . But for our Huguenot there
was temporary deliverance in sight. The prison of Lille was
under the orders of the Grand Provost of Flanders, a distant
connexion of a relation of the prisoner's: a tenuous lifeline
enough we may think nowadays, who know nothing of the
immense solidarity of seventeenth-century relationship. At any
rate, the claim was instantly recognized by the Provost to the
extent of moving his relation and a chosen companion into
a comfortable bed-sitting-room, with every alleviation of their
lot which money could provide; nor did his assistance end there,
for, having delayed their departure until the last draft, he then
had them carried in carts behind the chain to Dunkirk.
Marolles, another Huguenot, who in 1686 found himself in La
Tournelle, the Paris assembly-point, has a grimmer story to
tell; after complaining of the 'filthiness and execrable blasphemies' to which he is subjected, he goes on, 'We lie 53 of us
in a place which is not above 30 feet in length and 9 in breadth.
There lies on the right side of me a sick peasant, with his head
to my feet and his feet to my head. There is scarce one among

us who does not envy the condition of several dogs and horses';
and the conclusion of his letter to his wife is worthy to be
written in letters of gold—'When I reflect on the merciful providence of God towards me, I am ravished with admiration and
do evidently discover the secret steps of Providence which hath
formed me from my youth after a requisite manner to bear
what I suffer.'

At last the almost-wished-for day came when the chain
started on its long march to the Mediterranean; the weather
was cold and frosty, but the convicts, weakened by ill-usage and
burdened by their chains, sweated on the march. Charenton
was reached in the evening, and at nine o'clock the convicts were
ordered into the courtyard of an inn and made to strip naked—
ostensibly to search their clothing for contraband, actually to
steal from them their few poor remaining comforts. For two
hours they stood naked in the frost, and when ordered to move
were incapable of doing so, though 'the bull's sinew whips fell
like hail': As a result of the search eighteen of the convicts died
during the night. And so the ghastly march continued under
the lash of the archers. At night the convicts were locked in
stables, where the luckiest or the strongest proceeded to bury
themselves in the dung to keep warm, after dining off the 'King's
Bread'—literally the king's bread, 1½ lb. of it to each man.
By day the trail of blood left on the road would deceive travellers
into thinking there was a convoy of wine carts in front of them.
It may be objected that it was, at the lowest, the king's fuel
which was being wasted by this brutality: why were there not
regulations for getting it to Marseilles in consumable condition?
There were, but petty officialdom, our old friend the white
Babu, was active then as now, and the capitation grant had
been cut to a figure at which it cost more to bring a prisoner
alive to Marseilles in the hospital van than to let him die by
the roadside: and the result was that of every five who set out,
only four reached the coast, and of those four one had to be
sent to the galley hospital. If he was fortunate or unfortunate
enough to reach port alive, the *galérien* was sent to the depot
galley where he could make himself acquainted with the layout
of his future home.

The galley was in essence an open boat with makeshift
accommodation and storage space. We may picture it as having
about it a suggestion of the English canal barge—long for its

beam, with a freeboard of only three feet, and much smaller than one would gather from the pictures; about a hundred and forty feet long. Forward was a forecastle on which was mounted the ship's main armament, and aft of the forecastle a half-deck over the rower's space, which provided accommodation for the 120 marines. One mast was stepped through the forecastle right forward, and the other amidships: each mast carried a large lateen sail. Below the forecastle were some cubby holes and store-rooms. Fore and aft beneath the half-deck, and the complete length of the ship, ran the gangway from which the petty officers stimulated the exertions of the rowers. Aft was a poop, below which was a small cabin for the captain, and below the captain's cabin were store-rooms. The position of the other accommodations is not very clear—latrines, *Calle* or hold, where the marines slept, ship's kitchen, 'tavern' or wet canteen, a speculation of the chief petty officer: and I am inclined to suspect from various accounts that the interior layout of all galleys was not uniform. When these small craft were in commission there would be a complement of over 400 souls on board, and such was the overcrowding that even the captain's cabin was common to all officers except at night: for 'the cabin' was in fact the only real accommodation in the ship.

Soon after their arrival at the depot galley the convicts would be assembled, stripped, sorted into gangs of five, and drawn for by lot by the *Comites* of the various galleys needing reinforcements. Each five men, arbitrarily selected for physical reasons, were now entered into the closest of life partnerships, *La Vogue*: rarely again to eat, sleep, or work apart, to be literally in close contact with each other until the end of their days. They had ceased to be men, they had become 'an oar', one of fifty such oars carried by a galley.

But if they reached the port at the turn of the year, their rowing days were still three months ahead of them; the galleys, stripped to their hulls, would be emerging from their winter hibernation to face another commission. In this case the work in front of them was only one degree less arduous than that of the oar. No officers would yet have appeared on board, though a junior or two might be living ashore in the town. The seniors would be at Paris or Versailles, and the ships in the hands of the *Comites* and their *Sous-Comites*. The dictionary, I see, translates *Comite* 'boatswain', which is misleading, for there never was, thank God, an English version of the word. The *Comite* was the chief slave-driver, the man with the *nerf de bœuf* or bull-sinew whip. The first, indeed the only, qualification for a *Comite* was brutality; though even *Comites* varied, and the anonymous Huguenot whom I have already quoted found in his *Comite* a protector and almost a friend. We must not think too savagely of the *Comite*; only the exceptional man revolts against the abuses to which he has been brought up, and the *Comite*, had he been steam-minded, would have seen in himself nothing more than a chief engineer—half-speed ahead, one uses one's cane on the rowers' backs: full ahead one substitutes for the cane the bull-sinew whip. *Et voilà tout.* The galley in the early spring was a mere shell, there being little on board but the ballast, and fitting out began by removing this from the hold and washing it on the quayside. The lightened galley was then careened, scraped, and recoated with pitch. Then came the overhaul of the cables, anchors, rigging, sails, and the repair of the awnings, the last an important feature in the interior economy of the galley. Lastly, the guns, masts, ammunition, and a thousand and one other things must be carried down from the arsenal and stowed on board. About April, or later if the season was a bad one, the order would come from Versailles for the galleys to put to sea.

Life on board when the galley was at sea was a sort of Hell's picnic, for there was really no accommodation for anyone. For the convicts, there was, of course, no question of sleep; the petty officers did the best they could on the forecastle head, the soldiers huddled into the hold, or under the deck awning if the weather was fine, and even the officers had no sleeping-place except on their camp chairs under the poop awning. And so crank were the ships that, to avoid risk of capsizing, the awnings could only be spread in the finest weather. Cooking facilities were primitive, and, as no one ever washed, the ship crawled with vermin from stem to stern. From below came the constant clank of chains, the crack of whips on bare flesh, screams of pain, and savage growls. At each oar all five men must rise as one at each stroke, push the eighteen-feet oar forward, dip it in the water, and pull with all their force, dropping into a sitting position at the end of each stroke. 'One would not think', says a Huguenot convict, 'that it was possible to keep it up for half an hour, and yet I have rowed full out for twenty-four hours without pausing for a single moment.' On these occasions the rowers were fed on biscuit soaked in wine, thrust into their mouths by the *Comites* as they rowed. Those who died, or even who fainted at their posts, were cut adrift from the bench and flung overboard without further ceremony. But such a peak of suffering was never attained except in the heat of an action; had it been normal so to abuse the rowers, the whole criminal and Huguenot populations of France combined would soon have proved insufficient to keep the galleys in commission. In normal cruising, sail was set whenever possible, or, if there was no wind, only each alternate oar was pulled, so that each bench rested for 1½ hours in every three. Not all *galériens* were rowers; in each ship a few privileged men, who were usually Huguenots, would be employed as storekeepers, stewards, cooks, and the like. The only pleasant feature of this sorry story is the almost overt sympathy shown in most cases by Roman Catholic officers and *Comites* to the Huguenots; it was the comfortably lodged mission priests ashore in Marseilles and Dunkirk who were always on the lookout to make the Huguenots' lives harder, not the men who had to work with them. There were even cases in which something that might be called friendship sprang up between the captains and their convict secretaries and servants. Even the convicts proper, the criminal convicts, pitied and respected the Huguenots: and never failed, we are told, to address a Huguenot as *Monsieur* and pull off their bonnets when speaking to one.

In 1709 the hero of 'Willington's' narrative reached the haven of secretary to de Langeron, captain of his galley, and for the first time in eight years found himself freed from his chains, newly clothed, and allowed to grow his hair, with a corner of the storeroom to sleep in: nay, more, 'the captain ordered his steward to serve me a dish from his table at each meal, with a bottel of wine a day.... I was honoured and respected by the officers, loved and cherished by my captain'. This same de Langeron was prepared to take considerable risks for his Huguenots, though himself, of course, a Roman Catholic; when the search gun was fired from the flagship it was his duty to have each Huguenot instantly seized and searched for Protestant devotional books; but de Langeron would remark on hearing the gun to his steward—'My friend, the cock has crowed.' The steward ran forward with the news, and the *Comites* would look the other way before beginning their search whilst each Huguenot handed over his Bible to the Turkish headman of his oar. How real was the risk that de Langeron ran may be gauged by the case of Marolles's neighbour at the oar in 1686, 'a dragoon officer whose name was Bonvalet, a very mild and discreet man', who was there for life for having connived at the escape of a Huguenot woman of quality from France. Marolles, too, after the horrors of his journey from Paris to Marseilles, ultimately fell on his feet when posted to the galley *Magnifique*.

'I live at present all alone,' he writes, 'they bring me food from abroad (i.e. from the town) and I am furnished with wine in the galley for nothing, and with some of the King's bread. . . . I am treated with civility by all on board the galley, seeing that the officers visit me . . . we have the honestest *patron* of all the galleys. He treats me with all manner of civility and respect, and he hath promised me that when it is cold he will let me lie in his cabin.'

The privilege of getting food from ashore was a considerable one, for the diet of the *galériens* was, as might be imagined, spare. At eight in the morning an allowance of biscuit was issued for the day, 'of which indeed they have enough, and pretty good'. The only other meal was a soup made of beans or peas, with salad oil, at ten in the morning, to which when at sea there was added two-thirds of a pint of wine, morning and evening. Even during the campaigning season a galley spent much more time in port than at sea, and when in Marseilles or Dunkirk life was less hard for all concerned. Food was obtainable from the town, even by convicts, all of whom had some trade, and at night it was possible to sleep. Easily dismantled tables were erected over the convicts' benches for the officers and petty officers, on which they placed their beds, and each table became a sort of light tent by the aid of stuff curtains hung from a line fore and aft. It was then that a convict began to appreciate the privilege of rowing on the *Comite*'s own bench, if such was his good fortune; for the *Comite*'s table was built over that bench in port, and his men fed well on the leavings of his table: to say nothing of the prestige accruing from the enjoyment of the great man's conversation in his unbuttoned hours. 'He was', says our anonymous authority of his *Comite*, 'the cruellest man on duty I ever saw, but off duty very reasonable and filled with judicious thoughts.'

After the galleys came into port in the autumn and had been

laid up for the winter, the life of the convict became almost endurable. To begin with, the officers, sailors, and marines were billeted ashore, and there was much more elbow room, a general spreading out; beds were improvised in the bottom of the ship, and a huge cover on battens was pulled over the open deck, converting the ship into a sort of giant camping punt. Marolles on *La Fierce* found himself the possessor of one of the 'two little cabins at the head of the galley. This favour was procured me by a young officer whom I teach algebra. . . . I have bought coals, which are very dear, and I make a little fire in our apartment.' *La Fierce* must, however, have been a slack galley, for another convict, while commenting on the comparative comfort of winter quarters, adds that the chief drawback is that no fire is ever allowed in a galley in any circumstances.

Not only was the winter a time of comparative freedom, it was also the *galérien*'s commercial harvest during which he earned the money for his *menus plaisirs*. Every *galérien* had a trade; if he had no manual dexterity he knitted stockings; if he refused to learn to knit stockings he was flogged every day until he did. But it was only the lowest class of *galérien*, the submerged tenth, that knitted stockings; tailors, wig-makers, clock-menders, almost every trade was represented in the average galley. A week ashore was allowed by an ordinance of 1630 to the convicts of each galley in rotation, during which time they might freely peddle their wares and services through the town. Some were itinerant musicians and did well at the taverns, others hawked quack remedies, others set up stalls on the quay, others had good wig-making connexions, and all stole whatever they could lay their hands upon. For there was at least one advantage in being a *galérien*: there was no extradition from the galleys for any crime whatsoever: the criminal law had washed its hands of the man sent to the galleys. To be sure he might be flogged on board for a theft or a murder if the necessary social pressure could be brought to bear on his captain, but he could not be claimed by a magistrate for even the most flagrant crime. Hence the hideous scenes in Marseilles during the great plague under the Regency, when a more than usually fatuous minister inaugurated the brilliant scheme of releasing the *galériens* to help nurse the sick and dispose of the dead.

In addition to what may be somewhat loosely described as their honset tradesmen, the galleys supplied Marseilles and

Dunkirk during the winter months with a plentiful infusion of swindlers of every type: apparently without the naval authorities concerning themselves about the matter. The light-fingered gentlemen in fetters who wanted change for a crown and kept both crown and change: forgers of wills, marriage certificates, and leave passes for soldiers: dealers in the seals of towns, bishoprics, corporations, and private gentlemen: renovators and adapters of legal instruments—there was no need to look far in the port for skilled professional assistance in any fraud you might be planning. Indeed, Huguenots apart, the only tolerably honest men in the galleys were the Turks, who confined themselves to a safe conservative business as receivers of stolen goods.

Such in brief outline was the life of the galleys. There is a tendency, purely English, I suspect, to assume that because a man is ill-treated, he must be a good fellow; in our indignation against the whole system, we unconsciously draw a false picture of the *galérien*, on whom we need in fact waste no sympathy. The seventeenth-century criminal is not a sympathetic object, and his Huguenot fellows have left ample record of the horrors and atrocities which he boasted of having perpetrated. Whether the system made the criminal or the criminal made the system it is here irrelevant to inquire. It is all over now. The tumult and the shouting dies, the galley in all its gilded splendour and hidden misery has followed the age it symbolizes into oblivion. No more will French criminals 'write on the water with a pen eighteen feet long'. New horrors have displaced the old, but at least the bloody chapter of the oared navies is closed for ever.

BIBLIOGRAPHY

The Memoirs of a Protestant condemned to the Galleys of France for his Religion, Written by himself, &c., Griffiths and Dilly, London, 1758. Translated by 'James Willington' (O. Goldsmith).

Histoire de La Marine Française, vol. v., Charles de La Roncière, Paris, 1934.

Madeleine de Scudéry, Dorothy MacDougall, London, 1938.

Mme de Sévigné, *Lettres,* edit. Aimé Martin, Paris, 6 vols., 1876.

Evelyn's *Diary,* date 7 October 1644.

An History of the Sufferings of Mr. Lewis de Marolles and Mr. Isaac Le Fevre upon the Revocation, &c., J. Priestley, LL.D., F.R.S., Birmingham, 1738.

The Seventeenth Century, Jacques Boulenger, Heinemann, 1920.

Apostle of Charity, Theodore Maynard, Allen & Unwin Ltd., 1940.

Monsieur Vincent, Aumônier des Galères, Henri Lavedan, Paris, 1928.